VINKEN &
VAN TRICHT
50 BEER & CHEESE COMBINATIONS

www.lannoo.com

Register on our website, and we'll send you our regular newsletter full of information about new books, as well as attractive and exclusive special offers.

Text: Ben Vinken and Michel Van Tricht
Photography: Joris Luyten
Design/Layout: Android
Translation: Textcase, Utrecht
Translation for Textcase: Deon Everts

Special thanks to BOSKA for providing the slate cheese boards.

If you have any questions or comments, please contact the editorial team at redactielifestyle@lannoo.com

© Uitgeverij Lannoo nv, Tielt, 2012
D/2012/45/227 – NUR 447
ISBN: 978-94-014-0173-9

VINKEN & VAN TRICHT

50 BEER & CHEESE COMBINATIONS

LANNOO

BEER & CHEESE
OPENING UP A NEW WORLD OF FLAVOUR

Genuine foodies have long known that beer pairs better with cheese than wine. Red wine contains too much tannin overpowering the distinct cheese flavours and generally bringing out their worst. So it comes as no surprise that, in France, white wine is preferred as an accompaniment to cheese, since its lively acids combine better with the fats in the cheese. The same applies to beer. Sour, dry and re-fermented beer – in particular – cut through the fats in the cheese and make it lighter, cleansing the palate as it were, and allowing the taste buds to be more effective at their job. Cheese doesn't overpower beer, but joins it to create harmony or a defined contrast. We've known this for years, but it's time we dedicate a book to the topic.

A chance encounter at the foodie event 'Antwerpen proeft', where Michel Van Tricht had opened a superb cheese restaurant, led to this project and to a new friendship.

You're in for a treat every time you come across Michel. This craftsman, who virtually invented *affinage* in Belgium, is an extremely charming man and the ten tasting sessions that we held for the purpose of this book were indeed extremely enjoyable experiences. I would bring five types of beer, to which he would match the ideal cheeses. We weren't able to refer to any kind of handbook. All that we could follow was our collective flavour experience, acquired in practising our respective disciplines. In this book, we've set out to describe our combinations and the reasons for our pairings as effectively as possible without being overly scientific about it.

While working on the book, we also produced fifteen five-minute television episodes for Vitaya, each based on a combination from the book. These shoots took us to fifteen Belgian, French and Dutch breweries and cheese makers. These were idyllic days for us, with the world of beer opening up for Michel and the world of cheese opening up for me.

You'll find the results of these tasting sessions and our travels in this book, the first of its kind. It's been compiled in such a way that you're able to replace the cheese and beer from a certain combination with a different cheese or beer, related or made in the same style. You could, for instance, pair any Old Kriek with Stilton. It's all about the combination, not about the brand.

We wish you much tasting pleasure, and please enjoy the stunning photographs taken by Joris Luyten. They are a feast for the eye.

Combinations featured in the television programmes are indicated using this logo.

CONTENTS

AOP Appellation d'Origine Protegee / registered source name

PETRUS OUD BRUIN

The Bavik brewery is located in Bavikhove, Harelbeke in the centre of southwest Flanders, famous for its blended brews. The basic beer is a top-fermented brown beer that is further matured in oak vats. The vats at Bavik originally came from the Calvados region and were previously used to produce Calvados. Brewery owner Ignace De Brabandere recently ordered the installation of new vats, manufactured by a renowned local vat maker.

This beer became famous when the Petrus brand name adorned SV Waregem's football jerseys at precisely the time during which this club enjoyed its greatest success. Petrus currently sponsors the merged club of Zulte-Waregem.

Tasting

- **Origin:** *Bavik brewery / Bavikhove / Belgium*
- **Bottle:** *brown 33 cl apo bottle with crown cap*
- **Alcohol content:** *5.5% ABV*
- **Appearance:** *More dark brown than reddish brown in colour with a fairly firm off-white head that clings to the glass.*
- **Nose:** *Mildly sour, tones of lactic acid with a slight, fairly brief woodiness.*
- **Taste and aftertaste:** *Sour, but also tart and astringent. Dry, very well fermented so that the sourness, and especially malt bitterness, can set the tone. The aftertaste is short-lived and only the sharp bitterness remains in the mouth.*
- **Remark:** *As are all beers of the western Flemish reddish brown variety, Petrus is a blended brew consisting of wooden vat-matured beer (up to 20 months according to the label) and young top-fermented beer.*

Crottin de Chavignol AOP

This well-known goat's cheese comes from the Sancerre region in the Loire. The village of Chavignol has only 200 inhabitants, but is famous for its cheese. Crottin is farm-made, artisan product but it can also be manufactured commercially. A fresh Crottin weighs approximately 130 g. A ripe Crottin that has matured for four to five weeks is covered with a fungal rind that gives the cheese a nutty flavour. True experts even allow the cheese to ripen for four to five months. By the end of this period, the cheese weighs less than 50 g and, as a result, has a rich and concentrated flavour and a bluish tinge. Farm-made cheeses may only use fresh milk from a single farmer.

The 'super memé' farm-made Crottins, ripened by J. Bernaro, are of a very high quality. Dubois-Boulay in Sancerre is also well worth a visit. Here, Crottins de Chavignol are available at twenty different stages of ripeness.

Pairing

Michel found this a rewarding beer to combine with cheese. To create an elegant combination, he leaned towards sheep's or goats' milk cheeses. Eventually, he selected Crottin de Chavignol, a cheese that's ripened to a creamy texture in his atelier. This gives the cheese a 'freshness' that blends well with the lively beer.

Alternative: Clacbitou (and other matured goats' milk cheeses)

KRIEK CUVÉE RENÉ

Kriek Cuvee Rene, produced by the Lindemans brewery in Vlezenbeek, is an 'oude kriek', a brew that beer connoisseurs call 'the real thing'. This is not a Lambic with added cherry juice (like the sweet Lindemans Kriek), but a Lambic in which real cherries have macerated over a period of at least six months. The Lambic itself has an average maturation period of twelve months in oak. This is according to European standards, which must be complied with in order to use the term 'oude kriek'.

Tasting

- **Origin:** *Lindemans brewery / Vlezenbeek*
- **Bottle:** *75 cl champagne bottle with cork and crown cap*
- **Alcohol content:** *6% ABV*
- **Appearance:** *Its pink head confirms the presence of red fruit (cherries in this case) but, for a cherry beer, the colour is fairly dark and brownish with a reddish shine. Crystal clear is an exaggeration, but this beer is still fairly clear.*
- **Nose:** *The nose immediately betrays the fact that this beer is spontaneously fermented: sulphurous, cheesy with tones reminiscent of raw vegetables rather than fruit.*
- **Taste and aftertaste:** *This beer is very, very dry and borders on being astringent. Its sourness is described as tart by connoisseurs, so very sour! An expert in the field even reckons that this beer is reminiscent of genuine Schaerbeek cherries from thirty years ago, so this is the 'real stuff'. The aftertaste is brief and sour.*
- *Since 2005, the Lindemans brewery has had new vats in which the Cuvee Rene beers mature.*

Aged Stilton AOP

Stilton could virtually be described as the king of British cheeses. It is produced in the county of Nottinghamshire. Stilton is always made using pasteurised cow's milk. The use of this milk is enforced by the AOP, the Appelation d'origine protégée. After the cheese is drained and removed from its mould, the rind is smoothed using a pallet knife. Puncturing the rind with needles allows blue fungus to grow. If this takes place at a later stage, the taste of the cheese is more elegant.

Colston Basset is one of seven Stilton makers. This cheese maker distinguishes itself from other Stilton makers by using traditional animal rennet. Because the moulds are manually filled using ladles, the structure of the curd remains smooth and buttery. This cheese is at its best after four months of ripening. It then becomes pungent and matches sour, old-cherry beer very well.

Pairing

I discovered this pairing myself 'perchance' on a warm summer afternoon. I had uncorked a chilled Kriek Cuvee Rene and my wife had placed a chunk of aged stilton on the table to enjoy along with our dessert. I dared to combine the two and ended up seventh (flavour) heaven. To Michel, this was also a revelation. The fat in this complex cheese is beautifully complemented by the explicit sourness of the old cherry beer. What a treat! They're in perfect balance with one another.

Alternative: Bleu d'Auvergne, Bleu de Termignon

Hint: buy some pasteurised stilton from a regular retailer. Almost all stilton is pasteurised, although Michel can – of course – provide you with an unpasteurised version, though these are very hard to find. Such raw milk stilton is sold as 'Stichelton'.

ORVAL

Orval is an outsider amongst the trappist beers. It's the only trappist made using 'wild yeast'. This makes it characteristically sour. Of course, Orval is also famous for being very bitter, a result of the late dry hopping process during which large mesh bags of fresh hops blossoms are placed in the holding tanks like massive teabags. This process produces a tart and bitter beer that makes a great aperitif. If Orval is left to mature, ideally for two years, its sourness and bitterness become less pronounced and you're left with a smooth, but still very complex, beer that seems stronger than its 6.2% ABV.

Tasting

- *Origin: Abbaye de Notre Dame d'Orval*
- *Bottle: 33 cl skittle-shaped bottle with crown cap*
- *Alcohol content: 6.2% ABV (can increase with age)*
- *Appearance: Light amber, abundant off-white head that that changes to become unevenly structured.*
- *Nose: Although bitterness dominates, a lightly sour tone can be detected.*
- *Taste: On the palate, the bitterness also dominates, but in a very pleasant way. This bitterness is lasting – this beer isn't dry hopped for no reason.*

Pas de Rouge

This semi-hard cows' milk cheese, a 'paterskaas' or monk's cheese, originates from Ghent. The bacterium linens bacteria provide the stunning rich taste and colour of the rind. This cheese is washed in brine on a daily basis and ripens over a period of four to five weeks. The longer it's left to ripen, the stronger and more distinct its taste.

The 'Het Hinkelspel' cheese maker was founded in 1982 by three students who made cheese for fun. It has since developed into one of the leading Belgian traditional and organic cheese makers. Het Hinkelspel is a co-operative that purchases its milk from the Westhoek. It produces various types of cheese, including hard, herb, blue and goats' milk cheeses.

Pairing

Michel himself is a great fan of this unique beer. After a good pull on a two-and-a-half year old Orval (aged in the beer sommelier's cellars), he disappeared into his atelier and returned with a Pas de Rouge, a semi-hard cheese produced with raw milk by the Ghent cheese maker, Het Hinkelspel. This is a cheese with its own character that isn't overpowered by the beer, but that counters it well. Both products are complex, but not overly so. This is a most lively combination that works! It proves the point that it's possible to 'refine' or 'age' (certain) beers.

Alternative: St.Nectaire (and other semi-hard cow's milk cheeses)

OMER TRADITIONAL BLOND

This is a fairly new, warm-fermented lager beer from the category generally dominated by Duvel. The Bockor brewery in Bellegem has meanwhile won award after award, and it could be said that Duvel doesn't rule the roost anymore. This beer is somewhat fruitier. It's also smoother and does not provide Duvel's familiar tingling sensation on the tongue. One of the taste revelations of the past years.

Tasting

- *Bottle: 33 cl with crown cap and 75 cl with cork stopper (somewhat smoother in the latter)*
- *Alcohol content: 8% ABV*
- *Appearance: Gorgeous gold-blonde colour, pure white, thick head that clings to the glass.*
- *Nose: Fresh yeast that draws out the hops bitterness, somewhat more alcohol in the nose, making it reminiscent of Poire Williams.*
- *Taste and aftertaste: Malty, fruity and full of taste. Dry, delicately bitter and lasting aftertaste. Easy, drinkable, full-bodied lager that is very moreish. A true brewer's beer!*

Cabriolait

Cabriolait is a washed rind goats' milk cheese that makes for a unique combination. Its production method is identical to that of Pas de Rouge. However, its texture is somewhat drier, finer and less fatty. This is because of the smaller fat- and protein molecules in goats' milk.

The milk used for this cheese comes from white saanen goats crossed with alpine goats and is farm-delivered on a daily basis before being immediately processed. This method creates an extremely flavoursome product.
The red bacteria in the rind infuse the cheese, giving it a light hazelnut aroma and softening the end product.

Cabriolait is a product made by Het Hinkelspel that conforms to the strictest requirements with respect to health and the environment. This product is guaranteed to be free of preservatives and colorants and, during the production process, great care is taken to avoid the waste of ingredients and energy.

Pairing

Michel fell for this full and well-rounded taste. He decided that this beer needed a smooth, robust-tasting cheese. This led him to Cabriolait from Het Hinkelspel, the artisan cheese maker from Ghent. This is a goatcheese, made from raw milk, which Michel allows to ripen for at least three months so that it can lose some of its characteristic sourness. This is exactly what Omer needs. Strength versus strength, creating perfect harmony.

Alternative: Rigotte de Condrieu, Rouelle Cendré

TONGERLO PRIOR

© Wim Hendrix

This is one of the revelations from the past few years. This crème de la crème of beers only entered the market in 2009 as part of the Tongerlo range of abbey beers. Brewmaster Karel Vermeiren from the Haacht brewery in Boortmeerbeek worked on perfecting this beer for a long time. It is, after all, not easy to brew a good tripel. Thanks to fifteen years of experimenting, this is now perhaps one of the best tripels available.

Tasting

- *Alcohol content: 9% ABV*
- *Appearance: Golden yellow with a thick, white head that clings to the glass.*
- *Nose: An entire fruit bowl, with pear being dominant.*
- *Taste and aftertaste: Very full-bodied. This beer comes across as smooth, but then has a brief, very bitter – but not aggressive – aftertaste. It seems much lighter than the 9% ABV it claims to contain. Nice and dry, something completely different.*

Saint-Félicien 'Le Tentation'

Visit to Fromagerie l'Etoile du Vercors

This cheese is produced in St. Just de Claix, in the heart of La Drome, the region southwest of Lyon in the direction of Marseilles. For our television series, 'Vinken & Van Tricht', we visited the l'Etoile du Vercors cheese maker, where St. Felicien is made. It is a major operation, 'une grosse ferme', which produces around 25 million cheeses every year. We witnessed the entire production process, from the arrival and treatment of the fresh cows' milk to the 'empresurage', the addition of curd to milk in large tanks. Then on to the 'moulage', the spooning of the curdled mass into moulds, followed by 'salage' or salting and 'sechage', the drying of the cheese in special drying chambers in which the cheeses are constantly turned. The whole process takes four weeks: two days for production, six days for drying, and three weeks for maturation.

Why is it called 'le' Tentation, while everyone knows that it should be 'la'? Somewhere along the line, a moralist was involved and, to stop his constant nagging, they simply added the male article…

Pairing

This was Michel's first taste of a Tongerlo Prior, and this very smooth and fruity beer with its peary tones appealed to him. For this pairing, he provided a small treat. From his atelier, he brought an almost-runny 'spoon cheese'. It came packaged in a small round basket and he served it along with a spoon. It was a 'double crème au lait cru' from the Lyonnais region, another of those lesser-known food meccas. This pairing is an absolute gem. It is smooth versus smooth, and the beer blends beautifully with the cheese.

Alternative: Coulommiers

GRIMBERGEN GOUD

This is the latest beer to come from the Grimbergen family of abbey beers. The Grimbergen range is predominantly on the sweet side, except for the 'Goud' variant. This beer is distinctly dry-bitter and is, according to connoisseurs, the best Grimbergen in the range. During an initial tasting by the panel from Bierpassie Magazine, where beer is still tasted blind, most of the members believed that this beer came from a small brewery. Use is also made of Saaz hops, the best hops in the world. There are enough of this type of hops at the Alken brewery, where Cristal and this superb Grimbergen are brewed.

Tasting

- **Origin:** *Alken Maes brewery / Alken*
- **Bottle:** *33 cl with crown cap – bottle fermented*
- **Alcohol content:** *8% ABV*
- **Appearance:** *Pale blonde and cloudy; gradual carbonation with a fairly coarse head that clings to the glass.*
- **Nose:** *Fairly neutral with minty hops undertones reminiscent of pilsner. Is Cristal Alken perhaps brewed using the same type of hops?*
- **Taste and aftertaste:** *Refreshing, thirst-quenching and fairly bitter. Similarities to Duvel spring to mind, although this Grimbergen comes across as more full-bodied (alcohol content?), but has much less of a carbon dioxide tingle. Its aftertaste is fairly dry, fairly lasting and draws out into a slightly astringent bitterness.*

Le Petit Lathuy

In Werbomont in the heart of the Belgian Ardennes, the Fromagerie des Ardennes collects its milk from the nearby organic dairies. This milk is collected three times a week and is, therefore, very fresh. The cows that supply the milk graze on the Ardennes pastures and provide rich, high-quality milk that gives the cheese an extraordinary flavour.

Le Petit Lathuy is an organic soft cheese manufactured using raw cows' milk. It is circular in shape with a diameter of 12 cm, is 3 cm thick and weighs approximately 300 g.

The rind, with its white surface mould, consists of noble rot that forms during cellar ripening and is identical to that on camembert. This is a soft, creamy and delicate cheese.

The cheese is lightly salted. Its fat content amounts to 45 to 50% of solid content.

In 2004, this cheese was awarded the 'Coq de Cristal' at the Libramont agricultural, forestry and agri-food fair and was nominated the '2005 cheese of the year' during the Wallonia cheese competition held at Harze castle.

The Bioferme cheese maker is located in the eponymous town of Lathuy.

Pairing

Our cheese master found this to be a lively, brisk and dry beer. He quickly brought out the perfect cheese from his cheese-ripening atelier: Le Petit Lathuy, an organic cheese from the Ardennes made from raw milk and with a 50% fat content. The Fromagerie des Ardennes only uses unpasteurised milk and you can taste this. The cheese is rich, elegant and has a low salt content. It harmonises well with a fairly dry beer that elegantly cuts through this cheese with its beautiful white rind.

Alternative: Brie de Meaux

MORT SUBITE OUDE GEUZE

We previously tasted this oude geuze (Brussels beer) by Mort Subite for our 'Bier op hout (beer in wood)' series that was published in Bierpassie Magazine. This ancient lambic brewery has been in the hands of Alken-Maes for many years and, as such, forms part of the Heineken group. The age-old brewing technique of spontaneous fermentation is frowned on by some, but brewmaster Bruno Reinders need not worry about this. He is respected throughout his company due to the fact that he creates superb geuze's. Mort Subite is a 'first-time geuze', not too complex, yet with a very complex taste as a good oude geuze should have.

Tasting

- *Origin: Mort Subite brewery / Kobbegem*
- *Bottle: 75 cl champagne bottle with cork and muselet*
- *Alcohol content: 7% ABV*
- *Appearance: Amber coloured. Clarity varies between clear and cloudy as a result of bottle fermentation. Carbonation is gradual with extremely fine bubbles, head is fine and white.*
- *Nose: Typical lambic tones dominate, although fresh apple sourness is pronounced. There are also fruity tones and only a slight woodiness can be detected.*
- *Taste: Very little bitterness. Fine sourness dominates (mainly from the nose), reference to green apples but also to citrus fruits. Bone dry on the palate and the aftertaste virtually completely dries the mouth.*

Salers AOP

Salers is not only the name of the cheese, but also the name of the cattle species. These cattle, with their characteristic reddish brown skins, yield high-quality milk.
Just like Cantal and Laguiole, Salers has been produced in the Auvergne for 2000 years according to traditional methods. This cheese can only be made between May and October when the cattle are turned out to pasture. It's the only AOP cheese from France that is still produced on farms (app. 90), meaning that production is limited to around 25,000 cheeses a year. This farm-made cheese can be recognised by the red aluminium plate fixed to every cheese.

Salers 'haute montagne' is produced in one of the twenty 'burons' and comes highly recommended. This specific type of Salers has the most character with a rich, sweet, aromatic taste and an elegant sweetness. This cheese is at its best if left to mature for twelve months or more.
The Salers mass is not boiled but is ground between two presses.
This makes the structure of the cheese fairly coarse and this can lead to the growth of mould during ripening. This doesn't have to be removed, since it adds extra flavour.
A Salers cheese weighs 40 to 45 kg and approximately 1000 tons are produced every year.

Pairing

Michel was thrilled with this beer, since he is very fond of geuze. This was a fairly obvious pairing, because geuze marries well with cheese thanks to its high acidity. He brought out a Salers to go with this cracker of a beer.

Salers is a French, farm-made Cantal from the Auvergne made using unpasteurised cows' milk. It took its name from the medieval city of Salers and is recognisable by the red metal plate bearing the number of the farm on which it was produced.

Salers forms an elegant combination with the geuze. Its savoury, flinty taste (the Auvergne is volcanic) matches this complex yet approachable beer very well. This cheese was salted a second time. Perhaps that's the secret of this combination…

Alternative: Montgomery 's Cheddar

LA TRAPPE QUADRUPEL OAK AGED

The first trappist to be aged in oak comes from the Koningshoeven abbey brewery near Tilburg (Netherlands). This has been a daring initiative, but genuine beer enthusiasts have known for ages that time in oak makes a beer much more complex. The La Trappe brewmaster ages his strongest beer, the dark Quadrupel, in oak vats that were previously used for port. After two years, the beer is decanted into elegant 37.5 cl bottles with cork stoppers to make them even more special. This is an extremely exclusive beer that – like Westvleteren – is only available from the abbey shop.

Tasting

- *Origin: De Koningshoeven brewery / Tilburg / The Netherlands*
- *Bottle: 37.5 cl champagne bottle with champagne cork and muselet*
- *Alcohol content: 10% ABV*
- *Appearance: Crystal-clear to slightly cloudy (bottle fermented!), dark blonde but more amber in colour with a fine white head the clings to the glass.*
- *Nose: Pleasant fragrance with flowers in the starring role (it's as though you've walked into a florist), sweetish as a result of the alcohol (10%) and hints of vanilla from its time on oak.*
- *Taste and aftertaste: The flavour is pronounced. First a slight sweetness gathers that turns into a complexity that contains a harmony of flavours that are hard to define. No single flavour dominates. The beer is robust and full-bodied and creates a light tingling sensation in the tongue and palate. Its maturation in wood has clearly made this Quadrupel milder. The aftertaste is short-lived and a slight bitterness sets the tone. The warmth of the alcohol is prominent. You can, as it were, feel the beer 'sink'.*

Langres Fermier AOP

Langres is a washed, white cheese covered in a rind. It's produced in the Champagne-Ardennes, Lorraine and Burgundy regions. It comes in two sizes. The one more commonly sold weighs 150 g, while its older brother weighs 800 g. This cheese has an orange to light brown colour and is recognisable by its cylindrical shape and a hollow on top called the 'fontaine'. Sometimes a dash of Marc de Champagne is poured into this 'fontaine' to add extra flavour to the cheese and accelerate the ripening process, thereby producing a cheese within 20 to 25 days with a creamy and complex flavour and various different aromas. During ripening in the cheese maker, a mixture of brine and Rocou or Amatto is rubbed into the Langres. This process provides the cheese with a beautifully coloured rind in a natural way.

Most Langres are pasteurised, which sometimes gives it a superficial taste. Fortunately however, there are still farmsteads that make Langres according to the 'fabrication fermier au lait cru' method. Our favourite Langres is made by the Reillet farmstead in Genevrieres. This is one of the top Langres from the region.

Pairing

For this beer, Michel had to take a seat. I saw his eyes twinkle as he tasted it. I saw him enjoying it… and thinking about the right cheese. His unsurpassed knowledge of flavours led him to a classic from the Dijon region: the Langres, named after the eponymous town. This is a penicillium cheese that, according to age-old tradition, may be washed with Marc de Bourgogne during ripening. It's made using full-cream cows' milk and has a greasy, somewhat sticky rind that is dark orange in colour and has a penetrating smell. The cheese in the house of Van Tricht of course comes from a small 'fermier' and, with its distinctive character, creates the perfect balance with the smooth, complex, oak-aged and strong trappist. A combination of roasted malt, port and Marc… definitely one of the most intriguing and complex beer & cheese pairings in this book!

Alternative: Livarot

DUVEL

Some time ago, Michael Jackson called this beer 'a world classic'. This blonde, warm-fermented beer from Breendonk, with its characteristic 'spritz' on the tongue, conquered Belgium, as well as most of the world. Thanks to Duvel's success, the Moortgat family was able to be listed on the stock exchange and generate sufficient capital to realise explosive growth over the past ten years, acquiring breweries like Achouffe, Liefmans and De Koninck in the process.

But Duvel will forever remain the icon. You'll find it on every menu, even in restaurants and cafés where you'd least expect it.

Tasting

- **Origin:** *Duvel-Moortgat brewery, Breendonk*
- **Bottle:** *75 cl with cork stopper*
- **Alcohol content:** *8.5% ABV*
- **Appearance:** *Golden yellow, good carbonation, fairly coarse head that clings to the glass.*
- **Nose:** *You'll detect the pilsner malt, but also aromas of Saaz hops.*
- **Taste and aftertaste:** *Duvel is Duvel, a lively and extremely drinkable beer with a pleasant prickle on the tongue, 'definitely the Poire Williams of the beers' (according to Michael Jackson).*

Crémeux du Mont St. Michel

Now that various creamy cheeses from the Basse Normandy are being pasteurised, this traditional cheese remains the last farm-made, double crème, raw milk cheese from this region. It's made in Isigny-Le-Buat by Jean Charles Rabache. Its method of production is very similar to that of camembert. Once the cheese has drained in the mould, it's salted by hand. The cows that produce the milk for this cheese graze around Mont St. Michel on premium salé grass, giving the cheese a slightly salty flavour. It is ripened for twelve days before leaving the cheese maker.

Pairing

This beer immediately took control of our cheese master's taste buds. Its floral aroma and dry aftertaste quickly gave Michel the idea of combining it with a creamy cheese from Normandy, made on a farm close to the famous Mont St. Michel. Le Crèmeux du Mont St. Michel is a lively, almost playful cheese that perfectly blends with the dry, yet dynamic Duvel.

Alternative: Tomme d'Abondance

BUSH AMBRÉE

This beer needs no introduction. It is one of our strongest beers and, having celebrated its 75th anniversary a few years ago, forms part of our national beer heritage. Made of roasted malt that – in a special thick mash – creates the ingredients necessary to brew a beer with 12% alcohol. Sweet and sticky thanks to its alcohol content. What cheese could this beer be paired with?

Tasting

- **Origin:** *Dubuisson brewery / Pipaix – Leuze*
- **Bottle:** *33 cl*
- **Alcohol content:** *12% ABV*
- **Appearance:** *The head catches the eye in a positive way; the beer itself is amber coloured, clear and with a fine carbonation.*
- **Nose:** *This beer has a sultry aroma. On top of this, there are honey-sweet tones and a hint of liquorice.*
- **Taste and aftertaste:** *Sweet and liqueur-like; the alcohol is clearly discernible. It has a slight bitterness toward the end, but the aftertaste is mainly sweet with a distinct flavour of roasted malt in the throat. A beer to enjoy!*

Herve AOP

Herve is the best-known Belgian cheese and the only one with AOP-certification. During the 15th century, it was better known as Remoudou, derived from the verb 'remoudre', meaning 're-milking'. By applying the technique of 'remoudre', a farmer could pull the wool over the eyes of the taxman and landlord. Once they'd completed their inspections and departed, the farmer could 're-milk' the cows. Madeleine Hanssen from the Ferme du Vieux Moulin in Herve doesn't apply this method anymore. The Herve that she produces on her farm is made using full-cream raw milk. In her cellars, she ripens 'fromage au lait cru doux en piquant' with an 'affinage' of more than two months and a method called 'le palet du vieux Moulin lavé a la bière'. During the ripening process, the cheeses are washed in lightly salted water two to three times a week. The local yeast cells and bacteria, exclusive to the Herve region, give this unique semi-hard cheese its extraordinary flavour. This cheese is best served with wholemeal bread and Liege syrup.

Pairing

Time and time again, this beer has proved to be a symbol of the art of brewing, likewise to our cheese master. It had a profound effect on him, literally- and figuratively speaking. Such a blockbuster can only be paired with another Belgian symbol, the only raw milk Herve to still be produced in Belgium - made by Madam Madeleine from the farm Le Vieux Moulin in Herve, as you'd expect. Michel travels here in his van every week. This 'noble pourri' cheese dominates the sense of smell much more than it does the sense of taste. Served with Bush Ambrée, it creates a classy Walloon duo. 'A mourir', as the Walloons say…

Alternative: Maroilles

RODENBACH VINTAGE 2008

Every year, Rodenbach brewery reserves a limited edition for the American market, in which 'sour ales' (sour blended brews) are currently all the rage. An entire vat is bottled (around 20,000 75 cl bottles), and this is special single cask beer, meaning that it isn't adulterated with other beer as is normally the case at Rodenbach. We tasted the second release that contained beer brewed in 2008. Supremely smooth.

Tasting

- *Origin: Rodenbach brewery, Palm Breweries, Roeselare*
- *Alcohol content: 7% ABV*
- *Bottle: 75 cl champagne bottle with cork and muselet, stunning 'no label' look with transparent gold-imprinted label.*
- *Appearance: More reddish-amber than brown, crystal-clear, slightly cloudy and crowned with a beautiful, vanilla-coloured head.*
- *Nose: Lightly sour tones of balsamic vinegar, but also Madeira.*
- *Taste and aftertaste: a complex combination of acidities (lactic acid, malic acid) and esters (fruity), dominated by smooth sweetness, incredibly delicious and refreshing. Gets even better when you eat the right foods with it!*

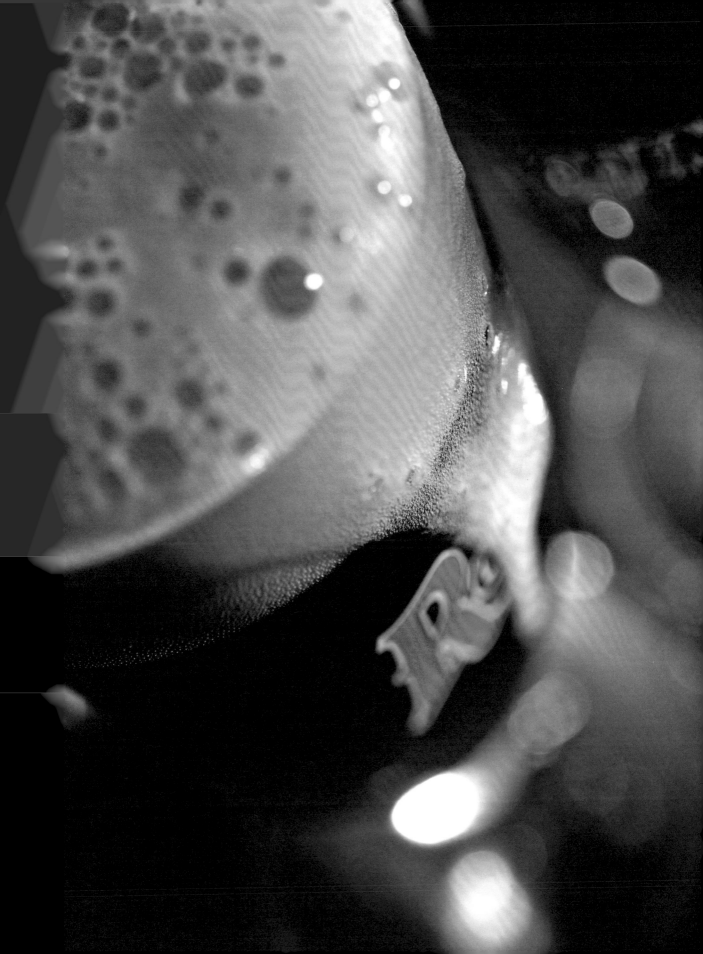

Brugge Cheese
matured in
Rodenbach

Visit to Rodenbach

While shooting our Vitaya television series, we visited the beer cathedral of Roeselare. This place has around three hundred 'foeders', imposing floor-to-ceiling oak vats. Rodenbach beer matures in these vats, and the contact between beer and wood produces lactic acid, giving it a vinous fragrance. This is the only brewery in the world to still employ genuine coopers, who maintain the vats, scrape off residue in preparation for new brews and repair the vats with straw and beeswax. This hall of vats is a place that should be preserved as a Unesco world heritage site. As you walk amongst the vats, you'll come across a wall with an inscription that reads 'The world's most refreshing beer'. This is a quote from the late Michael Jackson, who considered Rodenbach, with its invigorating sourness, to be the most refreshing beer in the world. Michel and I tasted this beer straight from the vat, a unique taste experience and one that was somewhat reminiscent of sherry…

Pairing

This is a semi-hard, creamy cheese that is ripened in the traditional old brown beer from Roeselare.
The cheese makers from Brugge Cheese went out in search of a unique processing method. During the ripening period, the cheese is dipped into an oak vat filled with classic Rodenbach beer.
In this way, the rich taste of the semi-hard, creamy and savoury cheese and the slightly sour fragrance of the combination-fermented Rodenbach beer combine to create Brugge Beer Cheese… The characteristic aroma of the old beer also infuses the rind, enhancing the culinary experience. On top of this, it gives the cheese a reddish hue (especially the rind) that makes for an attractive combination when placed next to a Rodenbach.

Alternative: Tomme Pyrenées Vache

ACHEL BLOND

The Achel trappist brewery, located along the Dutch border in North Limburg, has only been in existence for twelve years. To start with, it only produced vat beer but, after a few years, it outsourced bottling activities and – as a result – we can now taste a bottled brown or blonde version. The blonde clearly demonstrates its Westmalle DNA. It's brewed using Westmalle yeast and you can taste that.

Tasting

- *Origin: The Achelse Kluis trappist brewery, Achel*
- *Alcohol content: 8% ABV*
- *Bottle: 33 cl with crown cap*
- *Appearance: Stunning golden blonde colour with a thick, white head that clings to the glass.*
- *Nose: Extremely fine hops fragrance combined with sweet malt and floral, lively tones.*
- *Taste and aftertaste: After an initial sweetness, the hops bitterness sets in, after the rich taste follows a lingering aftertaste in which the bitterness is softened by velvety malt tones.*

Neufchâtel AOP

'Le plus vieux des fromages Normands' allege the cheese makers from the Pays de Bray in Normandy with pride. Neufchatel dates back to 1035 AD, but only became popular around 1800 when this cheese became available in and around Paris. These soft, mouldy cheeses are sold in various shapes. The 'Blonde' is cylindrical, the 'carre' is square and the 'coeur' is heart-shaped. We preferred the cylindrical Neufchatel from the Anselin cheese maker. Here, they use raw milk to make cheese with a velvety rind, which is perfectly ripened after five to six weeks. The rind provides extra flavour by combining its salty tones with melt-in-your-mouth pate.

Pairing

On taking his first swig, Michel endorsed the 'Westmalle DNA', although he found the Achel triple much smoother than the Westmalle one, a verdict upheld by the beer sommelier. A while later, he returned with a long basket and offered up an equally long Normandy cheese, clearly part of the Camembert family (but with more of a tendency to quickly 'run' out of its rind). This was the Anselin Neufchatel with its dark and uneven white fungal rind. It offered smoothness, saltiness, character and complexity. Definitely worthy of being married to a velvety tripel!

Alternative: Chaource

DELIRIUM TREMENS

Delirium Tremens falls into the 'strong blonde' category and is brewed by the Huyghe brewery in Melle in the Ghent district. It has enjoyed more foreign than local success, a point illustrated by a recent € 7 million investment in production equipment. This beer has a totally unique flavour that cannot be compared to other beers from this category, such as Duvel or Lucifer. The crazy name (meaning an advanced state of drunkenness) is also derived from the bar offering the most types of beer in Belgium, the Delirium Café in Brussels, which has now actually become a 'Delirium Village' in the Getrouwheidsgang just off the Grote Markt. Besides the one in Brussels, other Delirium Cafés have opened across the world with the most recent one being in Rio de Janeiro.

Tasting

- *Origin: Huyghe brewery, Melle*
- *Alcohol content: 9% ABV*
- *Appearance: Blonde, bubbly, fairly thin white head.*
- *Nose: Spicy (orange, lemon, fennel, aniseed, liquorice)*
- *Taste and aftertaste: Well-rounded and warm, alcoholic taste, yet with a slight bitterness in the fairly short-lived aftertaste.*

Vacherin Mont d'Or AOP

This seasonal cheese can be either Swiss- or French made. The French version is made from raw milk, while its Swiss counterpart is always pasteurised. It is AOP certified and comes from the Franche-Comté region. This cheese is available between early September and late March.

After being drained, the cheese is packed into pine rings to ripen and is washed in saline every day. The wooden rings give the cheese its characteristic flavour. In previous years, the cheese was made when the cattle were brought in from the pastures and yielded less and lower quality milk. Because many cows and much milk were needed in the Jura region to make the large comté wheels, people wanted a cheese that could be made quickly during winter. After all, winter milk was less suitable for the making of stored cheese. Hence, Mont d'Or was born.

Pairing

Michel had previously brought out this cheese to pair it with an earlier beer, but this didn't prove to be the right combination. It does, however, blend perfectly with Delirium Tremens. This raw cows' milk cheese from the French Jura must be eaten rind and all. Only then will you taste the actual flavour of the cheese, which packs enough of a punch to be paired with the sultry Delirium beer. Take note of the pine box. The cheese absorbs its resin aroma during ripening.

Alternative: Olivet Cendré (and other soft creamy cheeses)

GOUDEN CAROLUS XMAS

Gouden Carolus is one of the classics in the world of Belgian beer. The brewery in Mechelen that brews it dates back to 1379! Since the late 1990's, it's been managed by Charles Leclef, a descendant of the Van Breedam family of brewers who made this beer famous. It is characterised by its darkness, sweet malt flavour and a slight sourness. The Christmas version of this beer has all of these, and was nominated the best Christmas beer in 2010 during a tasting that we did for P-magazine. Gouden Carolus Classic (available year-round) is also perfectly suited to this cheese pairing!

Tasting

- **Origin:** *Het Anker brewery, Mechelen*
- **Bottle:** *75 cl with cork stopper*
- **Alcohol content:** *9% ABV*
- **Appearance:** *Dark brown and slightly cloudy, thick head that clings to the glass.*
- **Nose:** *Incredibly complex nose, initial wet grass and soil tones, hints of fine roasted malt emerge later.*
- **Taste and aftertaste:** *A beer that perfectly balances alcohol warmth, herbs, caramelised malt and that subtle characteristic Mechelen sourness.*

Gorgonzola AOP

This cheese, from northern Italy (Piedmont, Lombardy), falls under the protection of the AOP. AOP's are registered source names that are assigned to cheeses. This means that cheese makers that produce these cheeses must comply with certain regulations with respect to production, location, ripening, type of milk, animal species and weight.

Most gorgonzola cheeses are made using pasteurised cow's milk. The two versions are Dolce, which is creamy and smooth tasting, and Piccante, which is drained for longer, ripens over a longer period of time and is much more distinct in taste. The story behind this blue cheese is very similar to that of Roquefort, according to which a cowherd discovered mouldy cheese a few days after his cheese and leftover bread crumbs had mixed. This cheese weighs either six kg (Piccante) or twelve kg (Dolce). It was originally produced in the town of Gorgonzola when the cowherds would pass through and sell their milk here. The blue fungus is created by the addition of *Penecillium roqueforti* to the milk.

Pairing

Cheese master Van Tricht came around with a plate containing three Gorgonzola's, so he was confident about the type of cheese. We tasted two of these and the second Italian was perfect. It was a lovely, smooth, light blue-vein cheese with a fantastic aroma and a melt-in-your-mouth texture. The combination between this cheese and the slightly sour and spicy Christmas beer was to die for. A match made in heaven!

Alternative: Cabrales (or other soft blue cheese)

MALHEUR BRUT RESERVE

Malheur needs no introduction. This blonde beer from Buggenhout (the 10% ABV version) was the foundation on which the first 'bière brut' in the world was based. Brewer Manu De Landtsheer was indeed the first to be foolish enough to apply the entire champagne-making process to beer-making. All the way from primary fermentation to remuage and degorgement. It is brilliantly presented in a champagne bottle, carbonates perfectly and is bone-dry. A worthy challenge for our cheese master!

Tasting

- *Origin: De Landtsheer, Buggenhout*
- *Alcohol content: 11% ABV*
- *Appearance: Pale blonde with fine carbonation, just like real champagne. Thick, white head.*
- *Nose: Sheer hops blossoms combined with the fruity nose of green apples (granny smith) that give life to this strong, high-alcohol beer.*
- *Taste and aftertaste: The flavour is characterised by its dryness, pleasant bitterness and a slight alcoholic sweetness. The aftertaste is lingering, extremely dry on the palate and pleasantly bitter.*

La Gabarre

This stunning goat cheese with its gorgeous blue-grey fungal rind is made by the Ferme du Port Aubry. This means that it's farm-made using raw milk.

La Gabarre was the name of the boat used by the Berry peasants to transport their goats to Iles de la Loire. The shape of the cheese is based on the shape of the boat. The farmers hung bells around the necks of their goats in order to be able to find them again. This wasn't always all that simple, because the first hikers who came by boat to explore the islands took these bells as souvenirs.

Pairing

Michel had drunk this beer before and he remembered its bone-dry taste. This meant that it needed a dry cheese! From his atelier, he quickly brought out a La Gabarre, a dry goats' milk cheese made of raw goats' milk with a little added cream, something that makes this cheese very special. However, you'll really have to look hard for it, since it's very difficult to find. You don't have to be an expert to work out this pairing. These two fit one another like a glove fits a hand. Dry with dry, strength with strength, flavour with flavour… a simple, obvious combination, thanks to the great cheese master!

Alternative: Gratte Paille Affiné

LEIREKEN WITTE SPELT

This organic beer that the former co-owner of the Affligem brewery, Leo De Smedt, brews at Strubbe in Ichtegem is an outsider in the world of Belgian beers. It's a beer made with malt and spelt, a species of wheat that only thrives on very unfertile land. Because it is so resilient, this crop doesn't require any pesticide treatment. The resulting beer is reminiscent of white beer, but is something totally different. This is a fresh and summery organic beer. The name 'Leireken' refers to the Valeir, the engine driver on the old Antwerp to Douai railway line, now a cycling route in Flemish Brabant that still features a railway station and café in Steenhuffel.

Tasting

- *Origin: Strubbe brewery, Ichtegem*
- *Alcohol content: 5% ABV*
- *Appearance: straw-yellow colour, cloudy with a white head.*
- *Nose: Michael Jackson mentions dessert apples. Lemony could also be used to describe it.*
- *Taste and aftertaste: Fresh and fruity with hints of citrus fruit (lemon), prickling sensation on the tongue.*

Lingot de Cocagne

This is a soft and creamy sheep's milk cheese from the Tarn region in the south of France. At the start of its 'affinage', it is freshly sour, after which it becomes stronger tasting. This small cheese (100 g) is made from organic, raw milk. It is perfect after four weeks of ripening and swells out of its rind when cut. The literal translation, 'ingot of plenty' is therefore perhaps quite fitting.

Pairing

Was Michel influenced by the organic label on the Leireken beer? Whatever the case may be, he disappeared into his atelier and brought out an organic cheese from the Cocagne, made of pure, raw sheep's milk. A 'fromage de Brébis' with 45 % fat, hailing from the village of St. Antonin de Lacalin. This cheese looks beautiful, is orange-yellow in colour and has a thick, creamy texture. The cheese slightly dominates the beer, but why shouldn't it?

Alternative: Ecume de Wimereux

TIMMERMANS OUDE KRIEK

The oude kriek beer made by Timmermans brewery in Itterbeek was only released onto the market a few years ago. Not that Timmermans doesn't have a long history, but that – over the past few years – it has focused on commercial cherry beer, sweetened and made with lambic and cherry juice. However, a genuine, old cherry beer was absent from the range. Brewmaster Adriaensen first produces an old geuze in order to create an old cherry beer in which real cherries are ripened – or rather macerated – for six months in lambic that's one year old on average. The label features the old brewmasters of yesteryear (they are actually present-day co-workers dressed in period costumes…).

Tasting

- **Origin:** *Timmermans brewery, Itterbeek*
- **Alcohol content:** *5.5% ABV*
- **Appearance:** *Cherry red with a light pink head.*
- **Nose:** *Slight 'vat' fragrance.*
- **Taste and aftertaste:** *Distinct sourness that puckers the mouth (think 'Toxic Waste' sour candy). Somewhat nutty, only a slight hint of cherry in the aftertaste. Very refreshing. A beer that'll keep you busy.*
- **Hint:** *Allow this beer to age for a while and it'll become less astringent.*

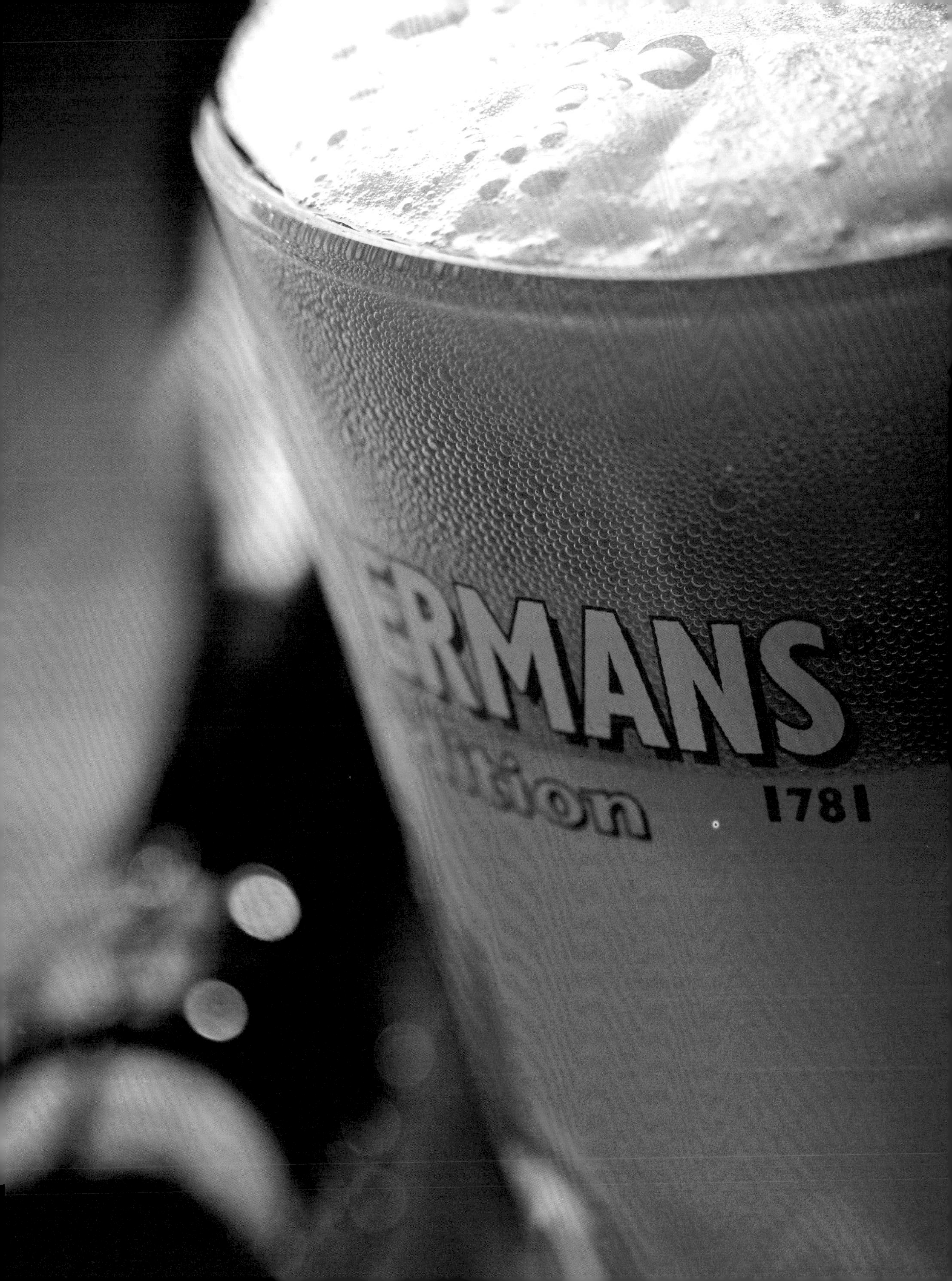
ERMANS
1781

Rossini Erborinato

Rossini's flavour is completely different to what you'd expect from a blue cheese. This is because it's ripened for three months in grape must from the passito grapes used for making pantelleria wine. During the ripening process, the amount of blue-vein bacteria increases. The crust also takes on some of the colour of the wine. The pasteurised cows' milk cheese is then pricked with needles to make the blue-vein bacteria develop. The wine also enters through these holes. This Lombardy cheese is produced by the Arrigoni cheese maker. Erborinato is Italian for blue-vein cheese. The taste of the cheese is pronounced but also sweet and is ideal for those less inclined to like traditional blue-vein cheeses.

Pairing

Michel stores around 350 different cheeses in his affinage atelier. One of these is this Rossini Erborinato from northern Italy with its greenish veins. At first glance, it looks a little dry, but once you remove it from its packaging, you'll discover grape skins. This cheese has been ripened for some time in grape must and vintners have clearly been involved. The cheese has strength, fattiness, character and simply takes on the fairly sour cherry beer. In a spot-on pairing, the cheese and the beer will complement one another.

This very special cheese from Bergamo (Tallegio) stands up to the onslaught of sourness, it softens the beer with its creamy fattiness and tastes delicious with it.

Alternative: Beenleigh Blue

LIEFMANS GOUDENBAND

This is a beer with a cult following made by the Liefmans brewery in Oudenaarde. This beer must be included on the menu of any bar that specialises in beer. It's a blend of old and young brown beer that is fermented and filled with Oudenaarde 'Brettanomyces' (wild yeast) in the brewery's open fermentation vats. We call this a beer of mixed fermentation, although it hasn't been exposed to oak and ageing takes place in sealed vats. When Duvel-Moortgat took over this soulless company in 2007, it injected new life into this beer. It's now beautifully packaged in a blue wrapper, something that the Liefmans brewery used when it started out as a prosperous company in 1950. Goudenband is a 'larder beer' and can therefore be stored for a long time. As long as 50 years!

Tasting

- **Origin:** *Liefmans, brewed in Breendonk, fermented and matured in Oudenaarde*
- **Bottle:** *75 cl champagne bottle without label but, unique to this brewery, wrapped in blue imprinted silky paper.*
- **Alcohol content:** *8% ABV*
- **Appearance:** *Reddish-brown and crystal clear with an off-white head.*
- **Nose:** *Malty and herby, rich in esters that make the nose quite fruity.*
- **Taste and aftertaste:** *Tingling freshness on the tongue, a perfect balance between lactic tones and the sweetness of roasted malt. Extremely well-balanced and complex beer. Lingering and slightly sour aftertaste.*

Torta de Oveja

This unique sheep's milk cheese tells a story of passion…

In Zamora, Spain, and close to beautiful Salamanca, there's a business that collects sheep's milk from farmers and exports it to France and Britain. This company's director, Fernando, comes from a family of cheese makers. He missed the art of cheese making and started a small cheese maker as a side-line to his milk business. He began by producing hard sheep's milk cheese in the Manchego style. A desire to make a creamy sheep's cheese took hold and, as a result, Torta was born. This raw milk cheese is actually related to the well-known Serra da Estrela from Portugal. The milk is curdled according to a vegetarian method, using the down from cardoon, a thistle that's part of the artichoke family. This specific rennet gives the cheese a lovely fresh and slightly sour flavour. The cheese comes wrapped in gauze that keeps its shape intact. The trick is to cut a hole in the rind and eat the delicious cheese with a spoon!

Pairing

This cheese from Salamanca, made from raw sheep's milk in the fromagerie Antiqua, has the creaminess as well as the sour streak that we needed to counter the complex Liefmans Goudenband.

Alternative: Bleu de Bresse (or other creamy blue cheese)

BRIGAND

This is the mighty blonde beer from Ingelmunster, home base of the former 'Brigands' or freedom fighters during the Napoleonic. It's one of my absolute favourites. This beer is handsome, lively, lightly hopped, full-bodied and has a sweet alcohol flavour. It is not for beginners. The Van Honsebrouck brewery is especially famous for its Kasteelbier, although this Brigand also deserves a high ranking. A totally underrated beer.

Tasting

- *Origin: Van Honsebrouck brewery, Ingelmunster*
- *Appearance: Golden blonde, with an attractive head that clings to the glass.*
- *Alcohol content: 9% ABV*
- *Nose: Strong, spiced and slightly bitter.*
- *Taste and aftertaste: Straightforward, full-bodied, hints of malt, coriander, cloves and orange peel.*

Chevrin

Chevrin is a white mouldy cheese made from raw goats' milk. The Gros Chene farm, owned by Daniel Cloots, is located in the fertile Ardennes, in the town of Mèan in the Condroz-Famenne region. This cheese is part of the Camembert family and weighs 250 g. Daniel has been making delicious, traditional cheeses – some of them organic – since 1976.

Pairing

Staying in Belgium, Michel placed an unknown, artisan cheese from the fromagerie Gros Chene in Méan in the Belgian Ardennes on the slate. This cheese is made using only raw milk and is reminiscent of Camembert, the white mouldy cheese. But this goats' milk cheese has much more 'power' than a classic Camembert. It holds up well to the strong beer and blends well with it.

Alternative: Cosne du Port Aubry

HOUBLON CHOUFFE
DOBBELEN IPA TRIPEL

What's in a name? Made by the d'Achouffe brasserie, this was the first 'IPA-beer' to emerge on the Belgian market. It was launched in 2006 as a kind of farewell gift to Chris Bauweraerts, because his brewery was taken over by Duvel-Moortgat in that same year. He was inspired by the American microbrewers that were more and more inclined to hop their beer, as well as by British troops who, in days gone by, took extra-hopped beer with them on their journeys to the overseas territories. The hops preserved the beer during the long voyages to the British colonies (IPA is short for India Pale Ale). The Chouffe version is based on the classic Chouffe, to which three types of hops – Amarillo, Tomahawk (both from the USA) and Saaz (from Bohemen, Czech Republic) – have been added.

Tasting

- *Origin: D'Achouffe brewery, Achouffe (now part of Duvel-Moortgat)*
- *Bottle: 75 cl champagne bottle with crown cap, bottle fermented or 33 cl (also available from the vat at a select few places, unbelievably delicious)*
- *Alcohol content: 9% ABV*
- *Appearance: This beer is even cloudier than a white beer. Its carbonation is gradual, although the white head is abundant.*
- *Nose: First impressions are of a citrusy spiciness and only later do the aromas of Amarillo, Tomahawk and Saaz hops become evident. There is also a hint of lactic acid.*
- *Taste and aftertaste: First impression is one of sweetness (due to the alcohol); its intense flavour and fullness mask the insistent and fairly sharp bitterness and create a certain balance. The aftertaste is lingering, dry and – of course – bitter.*

Munster Fermier AOP

During the 17th century, Benedictine monks from the Alsace in the southern part of the Vosges started making cheese.
The Munster place name is derived from the Latin 'monastrium', which means cloister. Another name used in the Vosges is Munster-Géromé. This well-known cheese has a light reddish colour. Its rind can sometimes be sticky and sweet with a pronounced flavour. The milk used is of high quality and is provided by Vosges cattle on a daily basis.

Ferme Minoux is located in the mountains at the foot of the Col du Bonhomme. This farm produces superb cheeses weighing approximately 600 g, or smaller versions weighing 200 g. These 'fromages au lait cru fermier' are delicious with boiled jacket potatoes. Munster with cumin is also a local delicacy.

Pairing

First Michel arrived with a Stinking Bishop. Coincidentally, I discovered this cheese during a beer dinner in the famous London pub, The White Horse in Parson's Green. Here, I sat with the late Michael Jackson and enjoyed this strong, smelly cheese that certainly lives up to its name. But I'd like to even go one step further in pairing the Houblon Chouffe. A Maroilles? Better, although this cheese has a bit of a 'one way' flavour and is somewhat one-dimensional. Not to worry, though, because Michel knows his stuff, and eventually he arrived with an artisan Munster from the Ferme Minoux, one of the few remaining non-pasteurised Munster cheeses. Both the beer and the cheese are 'power bombs' and complement one another perfectly. Few beers would be able to hold their own against this cheese, but Houblon Chouffe stands tall. It is bone-dry, and this is what the immensely strong cheese needs. The beer cuts through the cheese like a knife and, believe me, fireworks erupt inside your mouth. Be warned.

Alternative: A Filetta Brebis Corse

PETRUS GOUDEN TRIPEL

This beer with its noble name – reminiscent of a top wine – is the flagship brew of the Bavik brewery in Harelbeke, West-Flanders. It's a fresh and fruity tripel that always tastes good and, with its relatively low alcohol content, goes down easily. Petrus is known for a range of special beers, such as Bruin-Blond-Gouden Tripel, Oud Bruin and Aged Pale. However, the Gouden Tripel is its showpiece. This is no coincidence, since the Belgians became world players thanks to their superb tripels that acquire their complexity through bottle fermentation. 'Petrus, niet voor engeltjes (Petrus, not for angels)' is a fun advertising campaign that pokes fun at Duvel.

Tasting

- **Origin:** *Bavik brewery, Bavikhove*
- **Bottle:** *75 cl with cork stopper*
- **Alcohol content:** *7.5% ABV*
- **Nose:** *Quite neutral, slightly reminiscent of pilsner.*
- **Appearance:** *Pale blonde with a lovely white head*
- **Taste and aftertaste:** *Its taste is powerful, but also fruity and yeasty. Well-balanced beer with a dry, fresh aftertaste that lingers.*

Saint-Marcellin

Visit to 'l`Etoile du Vercors', makers of St. Marcellin

(also see 'Prior and St. Félicien', p. 24)

This small cheese made of raw milk is a product from the Dauphiné region. In times gone by, Tomme de Saint-Marcellin was made using goat's cheese. St. Marcellin can be farm-made, artisan, or commercially produced. It enjoys an 'affinage' of two to ten weeks or even more. Ezingeard's cheese is made on his farm in Auberives-en-Royans. Another cheese maker that produces these delicious cheeses using traditional methods is l`Etoile du Vercors, near the town of St. Marcellin in the Isère, at the foot of le Massif du Vercors. Every morning, this cheese maker collects rich and creamy milk from around one hundred selected farms.

Try St. Marcellin in a salad, warm or cold. A true delicacy!

Pairing

This spoon cheese, from the eponymous town in the Dauphiné and made from cows' milk, is incredibly creamy and gooey. This is something that really enhances the Petrus, with its hint of sourness. It only makes the beer better. What's unique about St. Marcellin is that, while in its mould, it only gets salted from the top. Then the freshly curded cheeses are taken to the drying cellar to further ripen and develop their flavour. Its delicate flavour places it somewhere between a ripe Camembert and a Saite-maure. Just like the beer, it's not too strong. This cheese comes packaged in a stoneware bowl from which you can spoon it out.

Alternative: Robiola 2 latti

MOINETTE BLONDE

We've now arrived at one of the favourites of the beer sommelier. Moinette Blonde is such a good beer that is, nonetheless, largely unknown and underrated amongst the general public. Of course, one doesn't need to convince beer connoisseurs regarding the qualities of this bone-dry beer from Henegouwen. It is brewed in the rich Saison tradition by the Dupont brewery in Tourpes near Doornik. What's unique about this brewery is the fact that its hops boilers are still fired by a direct flame, which caramelises the mash and adds to the taste. The brewer's wife also makes her own cheese using fresh milk from nearby farms.

Tasting

- **Origin:** *Dupont brewery, Toupes*
- **Bottle:** *75 cl with cork*
- **Alcohol content:** *8.5% ABV*
- **Appearance:** *Pale blonde and cloudy, lovely white head that clings to the glass.*
- **Nose:** *'Flowery' thanks to the hops, fresh.*
- **Taste and aftertaste:** *very fresh, bitter, but also full-bodied and fruity. It has it all.*

Vieux Moinette affiné à la bière

Visit to Dupont brewery/fromagerie

While filming this combination, Michel fell in love with the dry beer as well as the dry cheese. This brewery / cheese maker is situated in an idyllic village in Henegouwen, where time seems to have stood still. Every now and again, a cyclist or someone in a car comes by to collect beer. You'd have to be very well informed to find these fantastic products in the retail trade. Olivier and Pascale De Deycker are carrying forward their family traditions and continue to produce their delicious beer and cheese on a small scale. Our tasting took place in a typical village pub across from the brewery where we drank perhaps the best pilsner we'd had in our lives – Redor, a 'pur malt' and well-hopped pilsner. We spent the day reminiscing about times gone by.

Pairing

Here, of course, we were looking for a cheese from Pascale De Deycker's selection, made onsite in the cheese maker that's linked to the brewery. A delicate, matured, semi-hard cheese with a ripe colour sufficiently countered the lively hopped beer. Made for one another with love, just like the couple!

Alternative: Tomme de Savoie

PAUWEL KWAK

In contrast to the previous beer, this one is famous, even if only because of its eccentric coachman's glass on a wooden stand. Everyone is also familiar with the fun history of this beer that is brewed by Bosteels in Buggenhout. The coachmen, who in the time of Napoleon were not allowed to leave their coaches when they stopped at inns, would drink from their stirrup glasses that hung from the coaches. The beer itself is dark amber in colour with hints of roasted malt and a touch of bitterness, along with a somewhat higher alcohol content.

Tasting

- *Origin: Bosteels brewery, Buggenhout*
- *Bottle: 75 cl with cork stopper*
- *Alcohol content: 8.4% ABV*
- *Appearance: Deep amber colour, attractive head that clings to the glass.*
- *Nose: Smooth, sweetish aroma with spicy notes.*
- *Taste and aftertaste: Malty flavour with hints of liquorice, warm aftertaste that is reminiscent of caramelised banana.*

Cashel Blue

The Grubb family has been involved in the food industry in the Cashel area for generations. In previous times, they were millers. However, in 1930, Samuel Grubb purchased 150 hectares of land. After years of working in agricultural research, his son Louis returned to Tipperary to take over his father's business. He and his wife settled and sold milk commercially to the local creameries. Due to amendments in agricultural legislation, they decided to process their own milk into cheese, Louis' wife, Jane, had many years of cooking experience and she experimented with cheese-making on her cooker. She realised that there was no good Irish blue cheese available and decided to make Cashel Blue. This is a delicious, rich and creamy blue cheese with a hint of sharpness provided by the blue-vein bacteria. The milk used for this cheese is pasteurised and the rennet is vegetarian.

Pairing

This Irish pasteurised cheese with its blue veins and characteristic yellow colour (think Kerrygold butter) packs enough of a punch to be able to be paired with the Kwak beer that, given its higher alcohol content, can put up with a partner of substance.

Alternative: Blu Del Pian Rosa

CORSENDONK PATER

Jef Keersmaekers released this beer in 1982 and named it after the Corsendonk priory in Oud-Turnhout, formerly an Augustine monastery and now a popular conference centre. The Pater is a dubbele, while the Agnus is a tripel. This beer is brewed by the Du Bocq brewery in Purnode.

Tasting

- **Origin:** *Du Bocq brewery, Purnode*
- **Alcohol** *content: 7.5% ABV*
- **Appearance:** *Autumn-brown, attractive head that clings to the glass.*
- **Nose:** *Spicy and fruity.*
- **Taste and aftertaste:** *Spicy, pleasantly bitter with a slight dominant tone.*

Corsendonk Cheese

Visit to the Corsendonk Priory

To shoot material for our television series, we travelled to the Corsendonk Priory, beautifully situated in the Campine landscape. Jef Keersmaekers took us on a tour and told us about the history of this priory, which was famous for its scriptorium and library. We tasted the beer and cheese that bore the same name as a relaxing aperitif in the nearby 'Corsendonks hof', an inn that was a great place in which to enjoy the mild May sunshine.

Pairing

The creaminess of the cheese blends perfectly with this lively, untypical dubbel beer. It is rather dry and fruity and cuts through the fattiness of the cheese.

This creamy cheese comes from Gierle in the Antwerp Campine. It's made using full-cream, pasteurised cows' milk. This is a semi-hard monk's cheese produced on behalf of Belgomilk.

Alternative: Maggengo

GULDEN DRAAK

During an instalment of 'De Biersommelier' we paired this sultry and, dark beer with a Pas de Bleu, two Ghent regional products matched to one another. Gulden Draak is one of Belgium's strongest beers, and you must be in the right mood. But it's clearly a great beer to for gastronomic marriage, especially with blue cheeses. Brewed in Ertvelde by Van Steenberge, which has made inroads into the American market with this cracker of a beer that is – believe it or not – made with wine yeast!

Tasting

- **Origin:** *Van Steenberge brewery, Ertvelde*
- **Bottle:** *75 cl white-painted bottle with cork*
- **Alcohol content:** *10.5% ABV*
- **Appearance:** *Dark, almost black beer with a slight cloudiness and an attractive white head.*
- **Nose:** *Roasted malt, alcoholic sweetness.*
- **Taste and aftertaste:** *Sultry, thick and full-bodied beer, roasted flavour and a hint of bitterness in the aftertaste. A true blockbuster!*

Roquefort AOP

Roquefort is the most popular blue cheese to come out of France. After comté, this blue cheese is – in tonnage terms – the number two French cheese. The birthplace of Roquefort is found on a limestone mountain call the Combalou. The village of Roquefort is located on its northern slopes. All Roquefort's are made from raw sheep's milk sourced from the Aquitaine, Midi-Pyrenées, Languedoc-Roussillon, Alpes-Cotes d`Azur and Corsica regions. The AOP stipulates that all Roquefort's must be ripened in the natural caves of Mont Combalou in the Roquefort-Sur-Soulon district. They must spend at least three to four months here. Afterwards, the cheeses – weighing two to three kg – are pierced with needles and packed in aluminium foil to encourage the development of blue-vein bacteria. Look for Roquefort that doesn't contain too much salt and has enjoyed an 'affinage' of five or six months. The traditional 'La petite cave' cheeses made by cheese makers Vernières and Gabrielle Coulet are top-quality Roquefort's.

Pairing

A strong beer like this needs a cheese with serious pedigree. For this, we turned to Roquefort, the raw sheep's milk cheese injected with Penicillium roqueforti, which creates the mould and the famous blue veins. This combination approaches taste perfection. The sharp, sour and especially salty cheese remains elegant and creamy throughout. This cheese makes short work of the dark taste sensation from Ertvelde. Thanks to its five-week ripening period in Michel's atelier, is has the natural smoothness necessary to simply take on this beer with its 10% alcohol content. Roquefort 1, Ertvelde 0.

Alternative: La Peral Bleu

ADRIAAN BROUWER DARK GOLD

The late beer writer, Michael Jackson, was a great enthusiast of the 'Dobbele Bruine' made by the Roman brewery in Oudenaarde. Unfortunately, this beer disappeared from the scene during the 1990's, a great disappointment to the 'beerhunter'. It's a real pity that he's no longer with us because, in the meantime, Louis Roman's sons have come up with this stunning beer. They renamed it 'Adriaen Brouwer Dark Gold' after the famous medieval artist who lived in Oudenaarde.

In 2010, this beer won a number of accolades, including a Gold Medal at the European Beer Star Awards held in Nuremberg.

Tasting

- **Origin:** *Roman brewery / Mater*
- **Bottle:** *brown 75 cl Belgian bottle with champagne cork and muselet – bottle fermented*
- **Alcohol content:** *8.5% ABV*
- **Appearance:** *Dark amber in colour, crystal clear with off-white head.*
- **Nose:** *Very unassuming, but pleasant. A hint of caramel, a touch of spice and a dash of sourness thanks to the hops.*
- **Taste and aftertaste:** *The caramel sweetness is especially prominent in the mouth, along with a lightly roasted coffee bitterness. Still, there is a slightly sour and fresh note that ensures that the beer doesn't come across as sticky. This is actually a fairly simple, light and drinkable beer, despite its 8.5% ABV. The aftertaste is fairly short-lived with lightly roasted flavours.*

Brie de Melun AOP

Just like Brie de Meaux, Melun owes its name to a village in the Ile-de-France region, not far from Paris, the city of lights. The major difference between these two white mouldy cheeses is in the production method as well as the longer affinage enjoyed by the Melun. A Brie de Meaux weighs approximately 3 kg, while a Brie de Melun weighs around 700 g. This raw milk cheese contains more salt and is more fragrant. Brie de Meaux curdles in less than thirty minutes. Brie de Melun, in contrast, is curdled using lactic acid bacteria in a process that takes at least eighteen hours. On a well-ripened Melun, the white mouldy rind is overgrown with reddish-brown bacteria that give the cheese a strong fragrance.

Pairing

This soft white mouldy cheese is well-liked thanks to its creamy texture. This white mouldy cheese typically becomes overgrown with reddish-brown bacteria, which becomes even more abundant during ripening. We tasted this cows' milk cheese without its rind so that we could taste the strength – not the sharpness – necessary with the extremely smooth, refined and creamy beer. An elegant and silky-smooth combination.

Alternative: Feuille Dreux

BLANCHE DE NAMUR

Blanche de Namur is, in actual fact, the only Walloon equivalent of the famous Hoegaarden white beer. It is brewed by the Du Bocq brewery in Purnode, a brewery that mainly produces commissioned beer. It has the best systems at its disposal and simply uses these to brew an entire range of top beers. Two years ago, this beer won its category of the World Beer Award. In reality, Blance de Namur was an actual person. She was the eldest daughter of Jean I, count of Namen. In 1336, she became queen of Scandinavia through marriage and instilled French culture into Scandinavian society.

Tasting

- *Origin: Du Bocq brewery, Punode*
- *Alcohol content: 4.5% ABV*
- *Appearance: Pale blond, cloudy with a white head.*
- *Nose: Very floral (coriander dominates), hints of lactic acid in the nose.*
- *Taste and aftertaste: Much citrus flavour along with a crisp touch of wheat. Good balance between sweet and sour, making this beer easy to drink. The fruitiness and sweetness linger.*

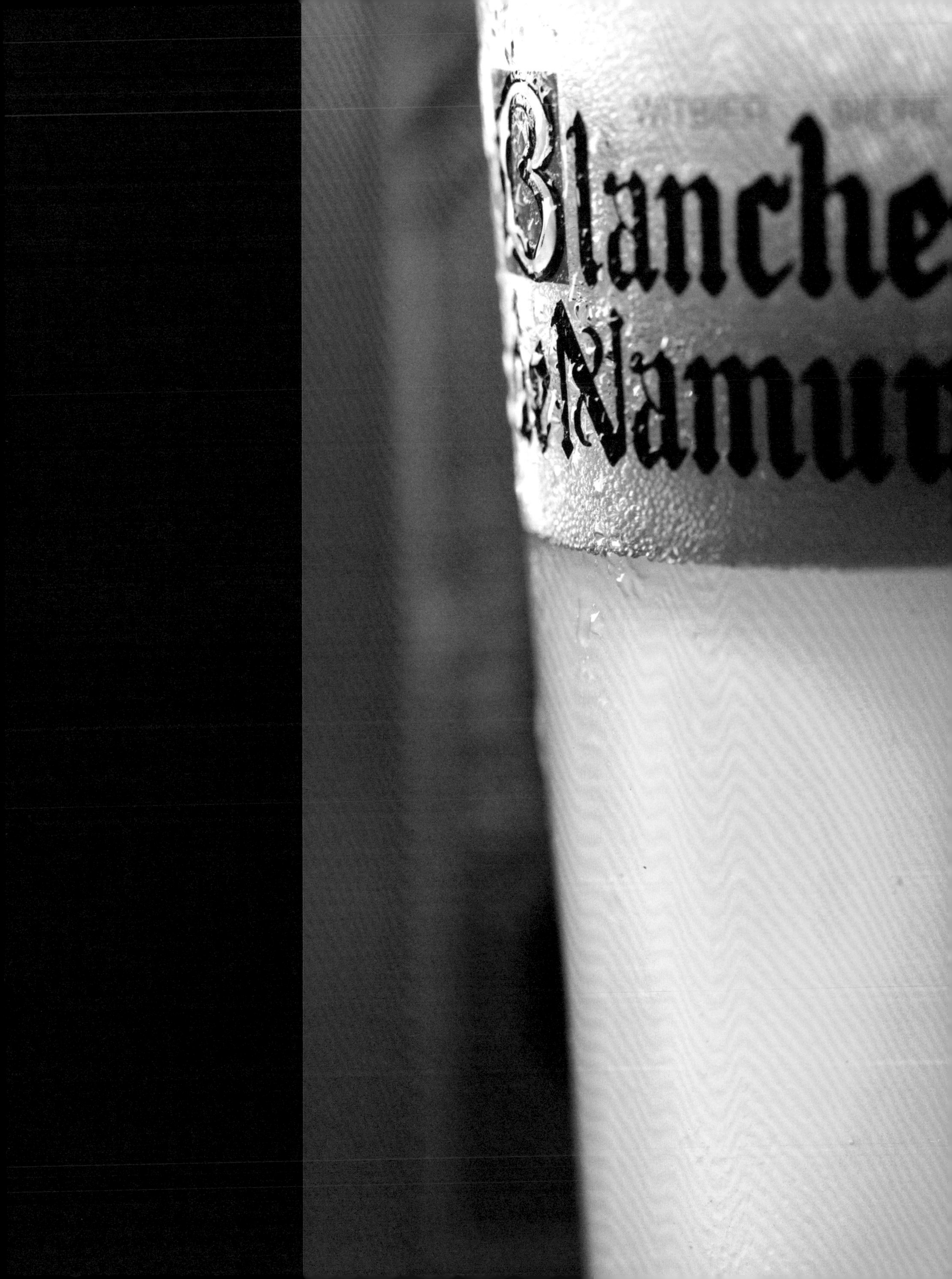
Blanche

Vanillien

Pairing

Michel had to find a cheese to match this playful and light beer with its tingling sensation on the tongue. He had developed a 'vanillien' himself as a new product concept. This is a cheese made from raw goats' milk sourced from a small farm with eighty goats in the village of Bajocasse, Normandy. In producing the cheese, three layers of vanilla powder are added and the cheese moulds filled over four stages. The cheese must then be meticulously aged. Only once it has ripened sufficiently (at least four weeks) will the balance be perfect. If the cheese is too young, the vanilla flavour will still be too pronounced.

Alternative: La Figue de Port Aubry

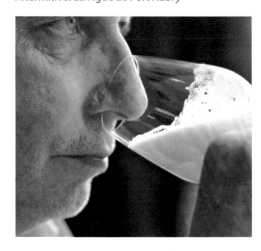 

ABBAYE DE FOREST BLONDE

The Silly brewery is a thriving family business in Enghien, Walloon-Brabant (not far beyond the language boundary). It brews pilsner as well as a range of specialist beers of which 'Double Enghien' and 'Scotch de Silly' are most famous. A few years ago, this brewery created its own version of a blonde abbey beer because it simply had to have one of these in its range, especially since it supplies around one hundred bars.

Tasting

- *Origin: Silly brewery, Silly*
- *Alcohol content: 6.5% ABV*
- *Appearance: Pale in colour, rich white head.*
- *Nose: Slightly fruity (poached pears?).*
- *Taste and aftertaste: Quite a tingling sensation on the tongue, refreshingly dry aftertaste. Fresh and thirst-quenching abbey beer.*

Le Petit Saint Point

Le Petit Saint-Point is a creamy cheese from the Franche-Comté region. Here, the fromagerie Michelin has a farm along the shores of a lake in the beautiful village of Point Lac. This is a delicate raw milk cheese that weighs around 300 g. Its rind is very soft and adds extra flavour to the smooth character of this delicate and creamy cheese. Petit Saint-Point is ideal for making a 'Tartiflette Jurasienne'. To serve 6 people, use 1.5 kg of potatoes, two Petit Saint-Points, onions, pepper and olive oil, following the recipe on the packaging.

Pairing

This raw milk cheese from the Jura can be consumed with or without its rind. The bitterness of the rind blends well with the bitterness of the beer. This is a light cheese & beer pairing that is generally best enjoyed at the start of a tasting.

Alternative: Le Petit Fiancé des Pyrenées

LEFFE BRUIN

The story behind Leffe started in 1952 with this beer. Brewer Albert Lootvoet concluded a royaltys agreement with the Norbertine monks from the Leffe abbey in Dinant. In return for royalties per hectolitre sold, he was permitted to use their name to brand his abbey beer. Trappist beers were brown at the time, so one of the first abbey beers had the same colour.

Today, thanks to the efforts of corporate giant AB Inbev, this is the bestselling abbey beer in the world, although the blonde version has taken the lead.

Tasting

- *Origin: AB Inbev brewery, Leuven*
- *Bottle: 33 cl or 75 cl with cork*
- *Alcohol content: 6.5% ABV*
- *Appearance: Autumn brown with a thick, latte-like head.*
- *Nose: Sweet, spicy.*
- *Taste and aftertaste: Full-bodied, sweet with a subtle bitterness in the aftertaste. Hints of vanilla, leather, preserved prunes, toffee and roasted malt. Well-balanced.*

Grevenbroecker

The Catharinadal dairy farm is located on the site where Franciscan nuns lived for centuries. It is at this farm, situated in Hamont-Achel in North-Limburg, that this cheese – also called Achelse Blauwe – is produced using traditional methods. This extra-creamy blue cheese, made from raw milk, was named the best regional cheese in Lyon in 2009. The top-quality milk comes from Meuse-Rhine-Issel cattle. This species, which is unfortunately on the verge of extinction, produces milk that ideally makes this cheese a unique product. The 75 MRI cows graze on the lovely meadows of a farm located three kilometres from Catharinadal. Bert manages the farm and his brother, Peter, manages the production of Grevenbroecker and 150 other cheeses. The weekly production of Grevenbroecker is limited to fifteen to seventeen cheeses weighing around four kilograms. This cheese is at its best once ripened for eight weeks.

Visit to the cheese farm in Achel

As part of our television series, we spent a day as guests on the Achel dairy farm. Brothers Peter and Bert Boonen manage cheese production and livestock farming respectively. The only milk that they can use to make their blue cheese comes from the Meuse-Rhine-Issel cattle species, which is unfortunately almost extinct due to low yield. In his strong North-Limburg accent (he's almost never left the village), Peter tells us everything about his flagship cheese, the Grevenbroecker or Achelse Blauwe. It's only made during winter and over the past twenty years he has perfected his own method. According to this method, the cheese is not injected, but the pieces of curd are placed on top of one another so that the blue-vein bacteria can develop with the help of *Penicillium Roqueforti*, giving the cheese its stunning marbled look.

Pairing

Achelse Blauwe, of which only fifteen rounds are made per week, has achieved cult status in Belgium. It is an extraordinarily delicious blue cheese, even more so when ripened in Michel's cellar. Michel didn't hesitate in selecting this cheese to pair with the brown Leffe. And he was spot-on. The cheese and the beer went down together with extreme ease as if they were a team. It simply works.

Alternative: Soumaintrain Berthaut

CHIMAY GRANDE RESERVE

We can only use superlatives to describe this reminder of the art of Belgian brewing. This Chimay trappist brewery has created a masterpiece, a stronger version of its dubbel or 'rouge'. It was originally released as a Christmas beer, but it received such praise that it became a permanent addition to the range. It tops the 'proef met Ben (taste with Ben)' sessions, and is virtually always one of the featured beers. Chimay DNA is evident in its meaty and smoky tones that are a result of the house yeast. It's absolutely world class.

Tasting

- *Origin: SA Bières de Chimay / Baileux*
- *Bottle: 75 cl Belgian bottle with champagne cork and blue muselet. Known as Chimay bleu in the 33 cl bottle. Bottle fermented.*
- *Alcohol content: 9% ABV*
- *Remark: This is one of the few – if not the only – Belgian beer that has a vintage.*
- *Appearance: Autumn brown, slightly cloudy and crowned with a fine off-white head.*
- *Nose: The 'house aroma' (smoky / meaty) is also present here. Fruit (overripe banana) dominates and is supplemented with sultry alcohol tones.*
- *Taste and aftertaste: Sweetness, reminiscent of dark chocolate, dominates bitterness in the mouth. The aftertaste is fairly short-lived, leaving behind a hint of roasted chicory.*

Sablé de Wissant

This is a cows' milk cheese from the village of Wierre Effroy in Pas de Calais in northern France. It is rolled in breadcrumbs, which more effectively preserves the aromas of the le Wissant white beer. It's made by the Bernard brothers, who have been making cheese since 1990. They only process raw milk and don't rear their own livestock. Their milk is sourced from two nearby farms and is processed warm. The pate is lightly savoury and doesn't have a pronounced flavour. During ripening, the cheeses are brushed with beer. This cheese maker is called Saint-Godeleine and it produces five other cheeses.

Pairing

Michel looked for a cheese worthy of marriage to this beer. He brought out the Sablé de Wissant, a raw cows' milk cheese from northern France, 'brossé a la bière blanche de Wissant'. The crusty 'sablé' layer consists of a type of breadcrumb coating that covers the rind. This is a cheese with much character, reminiscent of the cheeses produced by Chimay itself, since the abbey has its own cheese maker in nearby Baileul where the beer is bottled.

Alternative: Fort d'Ambleteuse

HOMMELBIER

Hommelbier is an extraordinary beer produced in the Westhoek. It's brewed by the Van Eecke brewery, located in Watou in the heart of the hops-producing region surrounding Poperinge. Watou is also famous for having the best beer restaurant in Belgium, Het Hommelhof. For many years, the Van Eecke brewery has been brewing a 7.5% ABV well-hopped beer, the Hommelbier. Hommel is the corrupted form of 'humulus', Latin for hops. This is a serious thirst-quencher because the hops ensure that it is very dry.

Tasting

- *Origin: Van Eecke brewery, Watou*
- *Bottle: 33 cl or 75 cl with cork*
- *Alcohol content: 7.5% ABV*
- *Appearance: Pale golden colour, attractive and finely structured head.*
- *Nose: Hops, malt and a hint of honey in its aroma.*
- *Taste: Very bitter and reasonably malty, a delicious, summery and dry outdoor beer.*

Beaufort Haut Alpage AOP

This impressive cheese weighs around forty kg. Its story is one of pure craftsmanship and tradition. To be allowed to use the term 'alpage', the milk must come from cattle that graze more than 1500 m above sea level. The vegetation at this altitude consists of a large variety of flowers, plants and herbs, meaning that the cattle yield top-quality milk that is rich in taste. The cheese is made between late May and September. Production is not possible during the rest of the year due to snow. The farmers actually herd the cattle into the mountains on foot. This cheese is made in small chalets and the initial 'affinage' also takes place in these chalets. Most of these cheeses are sold after a ripening period of one year, although it's ideal to ripen this cheese for two to three years because of the richness of the milk.

Pairing

For this dry, blonde beer, Michel brought one of his most expensive cheeses, the Beaufort Haut Alpage, from his cupboard. The cows that provide the milk for this cheese must graze high in the mountains and the cheese itself must be made at no less than 2000 m above sea level. During the summer, the animals graze on many flowers and herbs and one can taste this in the milk and the cheese. This type of gruyere from the Alpage (Switzerland), called L'Etivaz, also matches the beer perfectly. The dry beer elegantly cuts through the solid, fairly fatty cheese.

Alternative: Morbier

TEMPELIER

A few years ago, new life was breathed into Tempelier beer by Jef Keersmaekers from the Corsendonk brewery in Turnhout. He acquired the brand from a major brewery that had lost interest in it. In previous years (up until the mid-seventies), Tempelier was a strong, blonde, warm-fermented beer brewed by the De Sleutel brewery in Betekom. Today, a special reddish-brown beer with this brand-name is brewed by Du Bocq brewery by order of Keersmaekers.

He has taken his inspiration from the Italian 'birra rossa', although his beer is much more bitter and flavoursome than the Italian beer, which is normally too sweet.

Tasting

- *Origin: Du Bocq brewery, Purnode*
- *Bottle: 33 cl or 75 cl*
- *Alcohol content: 6% ABV*
- *Appearance: Copper coloured, with a luxurious white head (note: this beer carbonates well in its own mighty chalice adorned with the cross of the knights Templar, its coat of arms and two horses bearing Templar knights).*
- *Nose: Fresh, floral thanks to the Saaz hops.*
- *Taste: Full-bodied, fruity, with a clean, delicately bitter, dry aftertaste. Very refreshing and full of character, yet not too strong.*

Pelardon Fermier AOP

This goats' milk cheese from the Cevennes has been AOP certified since 2000. In contrast to many other cheeses, the larger part of production is performed by farmers and only a quarter is done by the major cheese-making co-operatives. The farmers use raw as well as unpasteurised milk. This cheese has a natural rind. After the curdling process, the curds are placed in moulds and drained. The cheese becomes lively and savoury after a ripening period of two weeks. It can also be dry-aged and can then be enjoyed when much older. The longer it is ripened the more flavour it has.

Pairing

This raw milk goats' milk cheese comes from the Gorges du Tarn in the Central Massif. It has a lively and elegant flavour, is savoury and is just strong enough to perfectly harmonise with the refreshing, not-too-strong beer.

Alternative: Pechegos

ST.FEUILLIEN BLONDE

St. Feuillien is a variety of abbey beers ranging from blonde, brown and tripel to Saison. Recently, even a 'Grand Cru' has been added to the selection. The blonde beer is now also brewed in Le Roeulx (formerly brewed by Du Bocq brewery) and walked away with the 2010 World Beer Award for the best pale abbey beer. Dominique Friart and her brother Benoit run this family brewery in the Bergen area. The blonde is bottle fermented. One clearly tastes the herb tones that make the Tripel so unique and this blonde is undoubtedly related. One can, however, drink more than a few of these. Apart from that, this herb flavour is a typical characteristic of many Walloon beers. On a past tour of Wallonia as part of a special feature for my Bierpassie magazine, I named this 'le goût Wallon'.

St. Feuillien is a brewery that we must keep an eye on. It cleverly anticipates trends in the beer market and succeeds in achieving success with limited available resources. I think that perhaps Dominique's feminine touch has something to do with this…

Tasting

- *Origin: St. Feuillien, Le Roeuix*
- *Bottle: 33 cl with crown cap*
- *Alcohol content: 6.5% ABV*
- *Appearance: Golden blonde, slightly cloudy, lovely white head.*
- *Nose: Hints of anise.*
- *Taste: Star anise continues into the flavour, although fresh body and elegant bitterness join in the mix. A spirited blonde.*

Perail des Cabasses

Perail is a fresh sheep's milk cheese made in the Aveyron, a region in the Midi-Pyrenees. This is an extremely soft cheese with a velvety, characteristic flavour. It ripens very quickly and is at its best after an 'affinage' of approximately fourteen days. The sheep from the Dombre farm in Verrieres graze in meadows that are 850 m above sea level. These raw sheep's milk cheeses weigh 150 g and are best stored under a 'cloche afromage' or on a plate covered with foil.

Pairing

Michel's cheese room yielded a 100 % sheep's milk cheese from Aveyron in France. Because it's made from raw milk, this cheese has a real farm flavour. It offers character, and this makes it the ideal match for the St. Feuillien Blonde.

Alternative: Rouelle Cendré

OUDE GEUZE BOON

'Oude Geuze' is a European registered trademark and can only be used to describe geuze (Brussels beer) made by blending lambic beers with a weighted average age of at least twelve months. What's more, this oldest of beer must be matured in wooden vats for at least three years. The secret of a good, aged geuze is therefore in its blending. In addition, the blend must undergo (spontaneous) fermentation in the bottle over a six-month period. The beer – brewed at its source with wheat and malt – is first spontaneously fermented in open fermentation vats and then further matures in oak vats for up to three years. During that time, the brewer must constantly taste the beer in the vats in order to create the perfect blend. And this is where the genius of Frank Boon comes into play. Not only has he amassed a large stock of vats over the years, he also succeeds in producing a 'mellow' geuze that can also be enjoyed by inexperienced geuze drinkers. Very few people today still enjoy an extremely sour beer, but no-one will refuse a mellow geuze!

Tasting

- **Origin:** *Boon brewery, Lembeek*
- **Bottle:** *37.5 cl or 75 cl with cork*
- **Alcohol content:** *5% ABV*
- **Appearance:** *Golden yellow, sparkling, lovely white head.*
- **Nose:** *Sour apples, characteristic aromas of brettanomyces (wild yeasts), a hint of wood, the genuine 'terroir' fragrance of the Pajottenland.*
- **Taste and aftertaste:** *Very mellow and drinkable geuze, yet still with sour and dry notes that linger in the mouth and give the beer a true champagne character.*

Brillat-Savarin

Henri Androuet developed Brillat Savarin during the 1930's. Henri and his son Pierre enjoyed great fame in French cheese circles. This cheese was called 'Brillat Savarin' as a tribute to 18th-century French gastronomist Jean Anthelme Brillat-Savarin thanks to his well-known quote that reads, 'A dessert without cheese is like a beautiful woman with only one eye'. This rich, creamy cheese has a 75 % solid fat content and a 32 % total mass fat content. Cream is added to the raw cows' milk. Brillat Savarin is produced in the Ile-de-France and Normandy regions. Royal Briard from the Seine et Marche region is a traditional Brillat Savarin made from raw milk.

Pairing

This dry and sour beer calls for a distinct, savoury cheese, and we found one in the Ile de France. Brillat Savarin is a farm-made cheese, and the beer cuts through it like a hot knife through butter.

Alternative: Dôme de Boulogne

WESTMALLE DUBBEL

This dark Westmalle is a classic trappist beer. It often serves as a representative for all abbey beers, because the balance between sweetness, malt and bitterness is sublime. It's an ideal gastronomic beer that marries particularly well with semi-hard cheeses, like those made by the monks, which are on sale at the Trappisten café across from the abbey.

Tasting

- *Origin: Trappisten van Westmalle brewery / Malle*
- *Bottle: brown 75 cl champagne bottle with champagne cork and brown muselet – bottle fermented*
- *Alcohol content: 7% ABV*
- *Appearance: Reddish-brown and crystal clear with a creamy light brown head – café latte, according to some. The head clings to the glass and is very stable in structure.*
- *Nose: Slightly fruity, although coffee bitterness due to roasted malt is prominent and is supplemented by hints of yeast.*
- *Taste and aftertaste: Because this beer is well-fermented, it contains little residual sugar. This makes it come across as somewhat one-dimensional (roasted malt bitterness and yeasty), but this makes it very drinkable or 'bekommlich', as the Germans would describe it. This bitter and dark trappist beer ends with a 'clean' aftertaste.*

Mimolette

It's believed that mimolette cheese originated in the Netherlands. Legend has it that, around the 17th century, France banned all imports of foreign goods. The French then started making mimolette themselves along the French/Belgian border in the Nord-Pas-De-Calais region. As a result, the cheese was renamed 'Boule de Lille'. The mimolette that we chose was a cheese that had enjoyed a fourteen-month 'affinage', also described as 'tres vieille' in French. The cheese is yellowy-orange in colour and sometimes red depending on its age. Most mimolettes are made from pasteurised milk, meaning that they're made by co-operatives. Older cheeses are ideal for crumbling and adding to various dishes. Blocks of mimolette in a salad also come highly recommended.

Pairing

Michel expertly matched this mimolette from northern France. The sweet tones of the Westmalle are elevated and enhanced by the strong and pronounced flavour of the 14-month old cheese. The rind of this cheese must constantly be brushed to remove cheese mites. Annatto (a South American colourant) is added to the milk to colour the entire cheese orange.

Alternative: Boeren Goudse Oplegkaas

KEIZER KAREL GOUD BLOND

On the occasion of the 500th anniversary of the birth of Emperor Charles, this beer – made by the Haacht brewery – received a complete makeover, its recipe was adapted and a perfect balance was created between the malt and sugary-caramel flavours and the hops dryness. A blonde counterpart couldn't be left out, given the major success of blonde beer on the beer market. You may not expect this from a pilsner brewer, but this is simply a delicious warm-fermented beer. Perhaps beer fanatics will find that it has too little character, because it isn't bottle-fermented and therefore lacks fruitiness. But the emperor was sure to have stopped his coach along dusty Flemish roads to drink this beer at an inn.

Tasting

- *Origin: Haacht brewery, Boortmeerbeek*
- *Bottle: 33 cl with crown cap or 75 cl with cork stopper*
- *Alcohol content: 8% ABV*
- *Appearance: Bright blonde, rich white head that clings to the glass.*
- *Nose: Fresh hints of malt and flowers.*
- *Taste and aftertaste: Full-bodied blonde beer with a touch of malty sweetness, slightly bitter towards the end.*

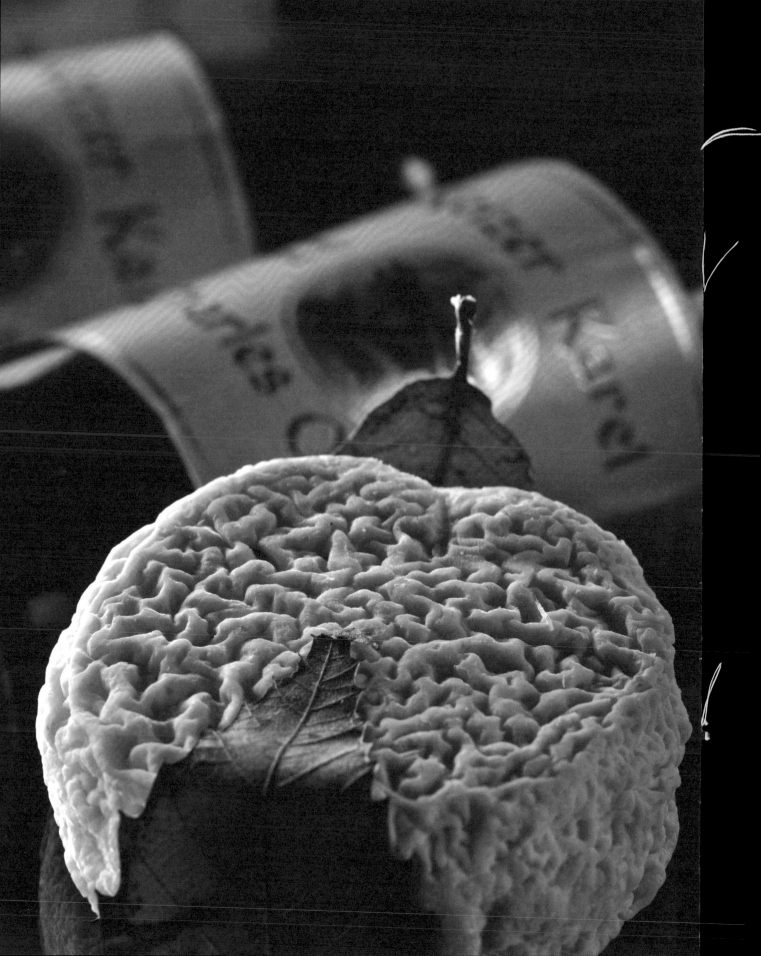

Mothais sur Feuille

This farm-made or artisan cheese comes from the Poitou region and is made from fresh, full-cream goats' milk. After being drained in its mould, the cheese is placed on a chestnut or plane tree leaf. This helps the cheese retain its moisture, enabling it to ripen differently and become more savoury. This cheese is at its best after three weeks.

Pairing

The fairly one-dimensional beer with its sweet alcoholic flavour blends well with this cheese, which originates from the Loire region and is farm-made using raw goats' milk.

Alternative: Torregio

CUVÉE DU CHATEAU

The brewmasters' experience came thanks to bottles of brown Kasteelbier that had been stored for ten years in the castle's subterranean cellars. After time, this beer had a flavour similar to Madeira/Port, and they wanted to achieve this effect by means of a regular brewing process. Hence the arrival of cuvee du chateau, a Kasteelbier based on the same ingredients but that – by means of a special, natural brewing process – also develops a 'port flavour'. Is this because less sugar is used? Is something added to the beer? Xavier Van Honsebrouck won't let the cat out of the bag – this will stay the brewer's secret. The fact remains that this Kasteelbier – a cracker at 11% ABV – tastes completely different. It's less sweet and more refined, but is still very strong. For those looking to find a wine in the same vein, try a Burgundy or a strong Médoc, such as a Pauillac.

Tasting

- *Origin: Van Honsebrouck, Ingelmunster*
- *Bottle: 75 cl with cork stopper, recently also became available in 33 cl bottles*
- *Alcohol content: 11% ABV*
- *Appearance: Dark brown, attractive white head that clings to the glass. Use the largest possible wineglasses and pour them halfway, just as you would a good wine.*
- *Nose: 'Aged' hints of Port and Madeira.*
- *Taste: These also come to the fore in the flavour, hints of roasted and caramelised malt with the subtle bitterness of fine English hops in the aftertaste.*

Epoisses Berthaut AOP

Visit to Epoisses

As part of our television series, we visited Epoisses Berthaut. It is located in the centre of the village and has a lovely story to it. After all, it was Marcel, the father of the current owner, Jean, who breathed new life into this cheese after the two world wars all but destroyed rural cheese making. Of the 300 Epoisses-makers present at the beginning of the 20th century, only two remained at the start of the 1950's. By 1956, there were none left. That is, until the Berthaut family got production back up and running. It takes around thirty hours to make an Epoisses because the curds form very slowly at a low temperature and with little rennet.

We weren't allowed to film this, because the process is so delicate that even the most minor bacterial infection would be fatal for the cheese. The transformation of Epoisses into 'le roi des fromages' is called 'Caillé lactique', which entails the development of fine flavours, aromas and acidity. The cheese receives 'neuf soins' – it's rubbed down with brine and Marc de Bourgogne nine times and only leaves the cheese maker after 35 days. During 'affinage', its rind changes in colour from yellow to red and – finally – it gets packaged in a small wooden box. Michel Van Tricht buys his Epoisses fairly young, since he prefers to ripen them for a few weeks in his atelier. We tasted an 85-days-old, runny Epoisses on location. A local chef made us a delicious sauce that, along with the cheese, we spread onto 'Boeuf Charolais'. We believe that God comes from France!

Pairing

The cheese that Michel chose for this pairing comes from the eponymous village in the Cote-d'Or in Burgundy. It's a very savoury cheese with a long history, a 'spoon cheese' made from raw and pasteurised cows' milk. It simply melts in your mouth along with the refreshingly sour, yet sweet and toasted, beer. Before it is ripened, the cheese is washed with a mixture of brine and Marc de Bourgogne. This gives it a unique flavour. Its exterior also changes from yellowy-orange to orange and finally, after a long ripening period, to brick-red.

Alternative: l'Ami du Chambertin

BRUGSE ZOT

Brugse Zot is a blond, fairly well-hopped beer brewed by Xavier Vanneste from the Halve Maan brewery at the Walplein in Bruges. This brewery has been in the hands of the Maes family for generations. Grandfather Henri Maes is still with us, and his daughter Véronique and her son Xavier breathed new life into the brewery after its return at the end of a long lease. They brewed Brugse Zot from the very start, since their traditional Straffe Hendrik brand had been acquired by another company. However, when Duvel-Moortgat took over Liefmans, the brand returned to Bruges. As a result, they now produce two major beer brands. Within five years, production had grown from nil to more than 20,000 hectolitres. As of recently, the brewery has a new bottling line in the Bruges industrial zone of Waggelwater. The beer itself is still brewed at the Halve Maan in the heart of Bruges, not far from the Minnewater. It features a great pub with its own courtyard where visitors can drink Brugse Zot in its unfiltered state straight from the vat, precisely as it should be done in a good home-brewery. Here, we tasted the filtered, bottled version.

Tasting

- *Origin: De Halve Maan, Brugge*
- *Bottle: 33 cl with crown cap or 75 cl with cork stopper*
- *Alcohol content: 6% ABV*
- *Appearance: Lovely blond colour with ample head.*
- *Nose: Pleasant hops fragrance.*
- *Taste and aftertaste: Fairly fruity with a pleasant bitterness.*

Pierre-qui-Vire

This soft cheese is made by the abbey in Burgundy that bears the same name. It uses raw, organic cows' milk. The rind of the cheese is lightly coloured with annatto, a natural colouring. A lovely, white mould then develops over this. The cheese pate is similar to that of a Chaource – a little chalky. Its texture is smooth just below the rind.

Pairing

This beer, with its floral nose, elegant aftertaste and pleasant bitterness, blends perfectly with this aged, raw cows' milk cheese from Burgundy. It's an abbey cheese with a rich flavour and the beer has sufficient body and strength to stand up to it.

Alternative: Soumaintrain de la Brie

HOEGAARDEN

Hoegaarden needs no introduction. It's always been the best white beer on the market, a fact consistently proven during repeated tastings. This brainchild of dairy farmer Pierre Celis (who passed away in April 2011 aged 86) that fell into the hands of AB Inbev (then still Interbrew), didn't do the brewing group any harm. Hoegaarden is enjoyed across the globe, although its name isn't pronounced correctly in most countries. This yellowy-white wheat beer encouraged many brewers to make their own versions of 'Belgian White Beer'. Belgian white beer is very different from Bavarian Weiss beer, which is brewed according to the Reinheitsgebot. The Belgians add herbs – mainly coriander and curacao (dried orange rind) – and these are what make the beer so delicious. A fruity and crisp sweet-sour thirst-quencher ideal for drinking on hot days.

Tasting

- *Origin: De Kluis brewery in Hoegaarden (AB Inbev)*
- *Bottle: 25 cl with crown cap or 75 cl with crown cap*
- *Alcohol content: 5% ABV*
- *Appearance: Yellowy-white colour with an abundant, white head.*
- *Taste and aftertaste: Hints of coriander and orange peel. Perfect balance between freshness and sweetness in the flavour. Lively summer thirst-quencher.*

Mont Ventoux

This little cheese bears the same name as the famous mountain with its snow-capped summit. 'Ventoux', which actually means snowy summit, explains why the lower half of the cheese is rolled in salted charcoal ash and the top half stays snowy white. It is farm-made from raw goats' milk and enjoys a ripening period of three weeks. When young, it is acidulous, though it becomes stronger, yet more elegant, as it ages.

Pairing

Michel served a fresh, cone-shaped goats' milk cheese from the Mont Ventoux area in southern France along with this refreshing, lemony beer. These two are a delicious match!

Alternative: Charpeau de Peyret

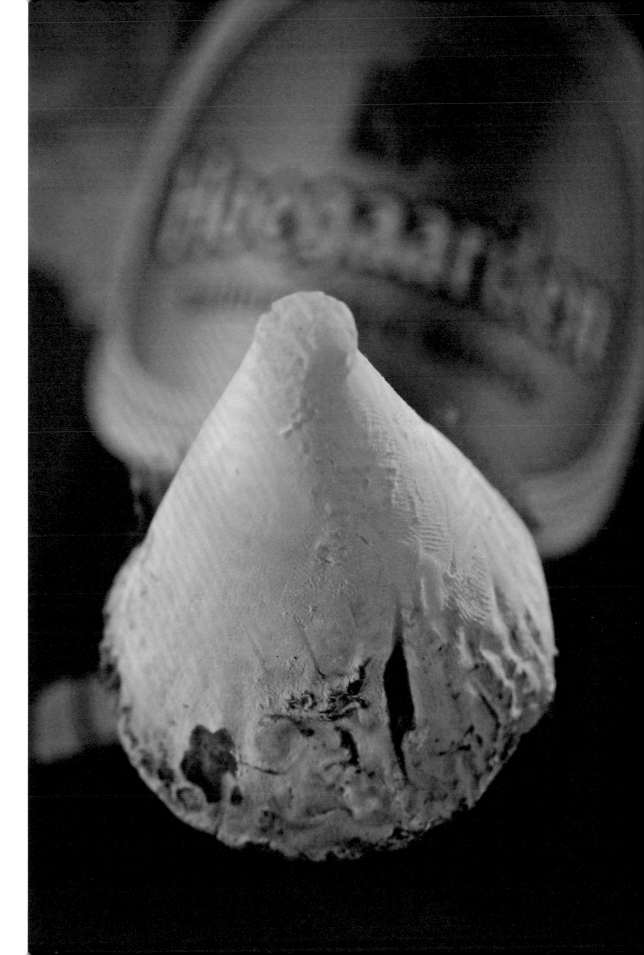

TROUBADOUR
MAGMA

For more than ten years, two young brewing researchers, Stefaan Soeteman and Kristof De Roo, have been brewing beer using the facilities at the Proefbrouwerij in Lochristi. Along with their mentor, Dirk Naudts, they developed a blonde and a dark Troubadour, both warm-fermented beers. The blonde has already won various prestigious prizes. In making their most recent beer, called Magma, they took inspiration from the success and revival of well-hopped beer, a trend that originated in the United States.

Tasting

- **Origin:** *Proefbrouwerij Lochristi, by order of The Musketeers, Ursel*
- **Alcohol content:** *9% ABV*
- **Appearance:** *Light yellowy-amber, orange colour with a rich white head that clings to the glass.*
- **Nose:** *Intoxicating aroma of exotic fruit, peach fragrances are also released when the beer is swirled.*
- **Taste and aftertaste:** *Full-bodied, strong and slightly sweet flavour. A lot of (poached?) fruit (rhubarb?). Bitter, herby and dry aftertaste that lingers. For true beer enthusiasts!*

Nuits d'Or

Nuits d'Or is a cheese from Burgundy with a washed rind. This pasteurised cows' milk cheese is related to Epoisses, but has a less powerful flavour. The cheese maker is located in Nuits-Saint-Georges and the cheeses leave the ripening cellars following an affinage of at least four weeks. This elegant cheese weighs 250 g and has a 50% solid fat content and a 25% total mass fat content. It tastes best once it has ripened for eight weeks.

Pairing

Its name, of course, reminds us of Nuits-Saint-Georges, the stunning winery village in the Burgundy region. The cheese is made from pasteurised cows' milk, is fairly savoury and has a coarse rind. This combination works well, because the dry beer needs fat to balance it out.

Alternative: Torta di Peghera

ROCHEFORT 8

The Notre-Dame de Saint-Remy Cistercian abbey in Rochefort is located in the stunning Famenne region and is one of the six trappist monasteries found in Belgium that still brew beer. This brewery only produces warm-fermented brown beers, the Rochefort 6, the 8 and the 10. The water that is used comes from La Tridaine, a spring located 42 m higher than the elevation of the brew house. The latter is definitely the most beautiful that you'll find in Belgium. It's a true copper sanctuary and, when a December 2010 news report spoke of a fire here, I was terrified that this gem would be destroyed…
Tall windows let in light that reflects off the shiny copper of the mash and boiler kettles, the original copper overflow trays sparkle in the bright light, the reddish-orange piping makes its way high up into the roof… It's a real pity that this brewery isn't open to the public.

Monks will always be monks, and here they also work discreetly and in silence. This is an abbey with a brewery, not a brewery with an abbey. The 6 is only served in the accommodation wing, although it is not a light beer. The number '6' indicates a 'Belgian percentage' and – from a normal alcohol content perspective – leans more towards 7.5%. The '8' (9.2% ABV) and the '10' (11.3% ABV) are the only available retail versions. Some time ago, we tasted an '8' from a 75 cl bottle that is bottled once a year for a local Lions club. Did you know that the characteristic Rochefort taste – it always reminds me of raisins – comes from the house yeast that was, until recently, supplied by a former Palm brewmaster, a certain Mr Carlier?

The Rochefort '8' is the most popular Rochefort. It's also the latest addition and was first brewed in 1954 as a Christmas beer. It was meant to be a one-off but, as is often the case, it did so well that it was later added to the fixed range. The same can be said about Chimay Bleu, which was also initially intended as a Christmas beer. Meanwhile, Rochefort 8 accounts for more than 54 % of total production. The '10' is indeed a cracker that packs a strong punch and was dubbed the 'cardinal of the trappists' at one stage. The '8' is more approachable and is also easier to pair with culinary dishes or with cheese.

Tasting

- *Origin: St-Remy abbey / Rochefort*
- *Bottle: 33 cl with crown cap, bottle fermented*
- *Alcohol content: 9,2% ABV*
- *Appearance: Autumn brown, slightly cloudy, topped with an off-white head that is finely creamy, stable in structure and clings to the glass.*
- *Nose: Sheer dark chocolate and raisins on rum, a chocolate panache - as it were. Its penetrating aroma suggests that this beer has a high alcohol content.*
- *Taste and aftertaste: Complex beer, the opposite of one-dimensional. Hints of Irish coffee, hops and coffee bitterness but also an alcoholic sweetness. A true winter warmer to sip in front of the hearth. Its aftertaste is lingering, alcoholic and bitter.*

Fourme d'Ambert AOP

Fourme d'Ambert has been AOP certified since 1976 and its production is therefore strictly regulated. This savoury blue cheese is made by major co-operatives as well as on farms. It is mild in taste when compared to Roquefort and is thus ideal for those who aren't all that enthusiastic about blue cheese. This cheese is made in the Auvergne region. It's a historic cheese that dates back to ancient Gallic times. To make this cheese, lactic acid bacteria, rennet and *Penecillium roqueforti* are added to milk. The latter makes the blue-vein bacteria develop. After the curdling process, the cheese is pressed into moulds and drained. Once removed from the moulds, the cheeses are washed in brine or dry-salted. They are then pierced with needles to encourage the interior growth of blue-vein bacteria.

Pairing

'Fourme' is an ancient word used to describe cheese, and it is still in use in the Auvergne. It was derived from the term for the moulds used to make cheese. This is a mild blue cheese made from raw or pasteurised cows' milk and has a grey or orange-brown rind. Its earthy and buttery flavours blend particularly well with the elegant, fruity and roasted beer that has great finesse.

Alternative: Bleu des Causses

WESTMALLE TRIPEL

Westmalle Tripel belongs in the top three on any beer menu. The Westmalle abbey has been in existence for 175 years and has brewed this exceptional tripel since 1935.

The fact that the Westmalle monks are conservative is a well-known secret. They run an 'abbey with a brewery' and not a 'brewery with an abbey'. Nonetheless, these monks are still highly involved in the brewery and the abbot and brother Benedict, in particular, keep a close eye on activities here. The latter – a trained architect – planned the entire new bottling plant and warm-fermentation chambers that are located underground so as not to disturb the cattle that graze above. These cattle provide milk that is processed into a semi-hard abbey cheese by the abbey's own cheese maker. This cheese is sold in the Trappisten café across from the abbey that, two years ago, was demolished and fully rebuilt in a modern style. The brewery, as well as the cheese making facilities, have the latest equipment at their disposal. The monks' sole objective is – after all – quality, quality and quality again. Money is not an issue here. The Tripel is undoubtedly their best beer, and is perhaps simply the best beer available. It was also the first tripel produced in the world, albeit according to the recipe of Henri Vanderlinden, the brewer at nearby Witkap in Brasschaat and a former advisor to this brewery. Many tripels were to follow, one better than the next, but a true Antwerp Campine native will only drink a Westmalle tripel. The abbey has worked hard to consistently make this beer so good, although Brother Benedict compares this to the abbey's canon hymns that took hundreds of years to perfect. The best things in life take time.

Tasting

- **Origin:** *Our Dear Lady of Westmalle abbey*
- **Alcohol content:** *9.5% ABV*
- **Bottle:** *33 cl with crown cap (also available in 75 cl bottle with cork stopper, somewhat smoother and with a hint of vanilla in this format)*
- **Appearance:** *Golden blonde, with astonishingly fine carbonation and a white, creamy, fine and abundant head.*
- **Nose:** *Very fruity (overripe banana), along with a malty flavour and slight bitterness.*
- **Taste:** *This beer is delicately sweet on the tongue without being sticky. Its aftertaste is pleasantly bitter.*

Li P'tit Rossê

Li P'tit Rossê is a lovely cheese with a washed rind that comes from the heart of the Ardennes. Fromagerie des Ardennes in Werbomont, established in 1996, purchased a new building called '7 days'. This building is only used for the making of traditional cheeses, using superior-quality milk, which can be labelled as organic. This is all in order to comply with ever-stricter European standards. This is a strong cheese made from raw, organic cows' milk that weighs in at 180 g. Its taste is reminiscent of a soft herve cheese. The orange-coloured rind that is covered in a white downy substance is the result of the growth of a variety of bacteria.

Pairing

Of course, the Westmalle house cheese tastes great with the beer, but Michel wouldn't be Michel if he didn't work his magic by pairing the beer with something from his atelier. He brought out a Le P'tit Rosse, a Belgian organic cheese made with fresh milk and produced by the Fromagerie des Ardennes in Werbomont.

Alternative: Carré Corse

TRIPEL KARMELIET

Tripel Karmeliet is currently one of the most popular tripels. The Bosteels brewery in Buggenhout created this beer in 1997 and I had the privilege of tasting the first brew in the company of the 'beerhunter', Michael Jackson. It's a triple-grain beer (malt, wheat, oats) brewed according to a recipe from the Dendermonde Carmelite monastery that Antoine Bosteels was fortunate enough to lay his hands on. This beer is characterised by a lemony aroma and its superb drinkability. A winner at any beer festival.

Tasting

- *Origin: Bosteels brewery, Buggenhout*
- *Bottle: 33 cl with crown cap or 75 cl with cork stopper.*
- *Alcohol content: 8% ABV*
- *Appearance: Stunning, golden yellow colour with a lovely white head.*
- *Nose: Fruit (peaches, apricots, lemons) and cloves.*
- *Taste: Mild-flavoured, leaning towards sweet. Still refreshing and drinkable.*

Comté Fort St. Antoine AOP

Comté is a cheese from the Jura that is the most widely-produced cheese in France. Comté cheese wheels weigh around 35 kg and are always made from raw milk. Marcel Petite owns two different ripening centres. In Graces-Narboz, a village near Pontalier, the comtés are ripened after being made using milk from cattle that graze at an altitude of no less than 600 m.

Fort Saint Antoine is an old military fort that dates back to the mid-19th century and lies at an altitude of 1100 m. It is in this stunning fort that the Comté des Montagnes ripen. The milk provided by the cattle is of high quality because they graze in high mountain pastures with a variety of plants, herbs and flowers. This yields rich and creamy milk. The cheeses don't leave the fort before they've enjoyed an 'affinage' of fourteen months, during which they're inspected every day by specialist comté experts. The better comtés are marked with green bands in order to distinguish them from those with small defects. The latter are marked with brown bands.

It's best to buy Comté as a whole block. Offcuts of this superb cheese suffer a loss of flavour and aroma.

Visit to Fort Fort St. Antoine

Michel was able to arrange a visit to this exclusive cheese sanctuary for the purpose of our television programme. This fort holds ten thousand ripening comté wheels. It has vast hallways filled with these impressive cheeses that are regularly turned by robots. The cheese is only ripened here, and is made and delivered by the 'fruitières' in the area, the cheese makers that collect the milk from farms in the region. This truly is a breath-taking area, the Jura in the Franche-Comté being one of the most stunning parts of France. The border with Switzerland consists of a massive mountain range. This is untouched nature, and you can taste that in the fruity cheese. The best comtés ripen for at least one year.

Pairing

This is a great visual pairing, because both the cheese and the beer have a natural yellow colour. However, the fruitiness of the cheese (the cattle graze on flowers in the Jura alpine pastures) and the fruitiness of the beer complement one another wonderfully and their floral tones meet here. A brilliant pairing!

Alternative: Quartirolo Lombardo

BOURGOGNE DES FLANDRES

Bourgogne des Flandres is a dark brown beer that was previously brewed by the now defunct Van Houtryve brewery in Bruges. This beer, a blend of dark, warm-fermented ale and spontaneously fermented lambic, was brewed for some time by the Verhaeghe brewery in Vichte, but lost the brand to the Anthony Martin liquor group. This company now brews the beer in its Timmermans lambic brewery, where – after all – they have a great deal of experience in blending beer.

Tasting

- *Origin: Timmermans brewery, Itterbeek*
- *Bottle: 33 cl with crown cap*
- *Alcohol content: 5% ABV*
- *Appearance: Dark brown, with a fine head that clings to the glass.*
- *Nose: Sharp woody and acidic aroma, but with a hint of sweetness.*
- *Taste and aftertaste: Sweetly-sour and complex, although surprisingly drinkable with a short-lived aftertaste.*

Maconnais AOP

Maconnais is a small cheese from the Macon region in Burgundy. These cheeses only weigh between 50 g and 60 g and ripen beautifully, acquiring a lovely, natural mouldy rind in the process. Maconnais is a goats' milk cheese made from raw milk. These cheeses can be artisan or farm-made. If a farm makes cheese only using milk from its own goats, such cheese is 'fermier' cheese. If milk is purchased from other farms, it becomes 'artisan' maconnais. The Chevenet cheese maker in the charming village of Hurigny makes fantastic Maconnais cheeses that are a true delicacy, whether they're fresh (two-week 'affinage') or well-ripened. We also recommend that you try this cheese in salad or baked on bread in the oven.

Visit to Maconnais

As part of our television series, we were hosted by Thierry and Nathalie Chevenet who are young, hardworking people who make lovely products. Thierry loves his five thousand goats that provide the fresh milk with which the cheese is made. As the cheeses ripen, they acquire a natural blue mould the colour of the grapes used to make Macon-Villages on the same farm. A month before our visit, around fifteen hundred kids were born, meaning that this is the time during which the goats yield the most milk. Approximately half a litre of milk is required for a single cheese.

Pairing

To pair with this beer from Burgundy (at one time, Bruges was the capital of Burgundy!), Michel selected a superb goats' milk cheese from, well... southern Burgundy. In Hurigny, the Chevenet family runs a farm that produces cheese as well as wine. The cheese is made from raw goats' milk and the goats are reared on the farm. This dry, fresh cheese is a fantastic match for the sour-sweet beer.

Alternative: Briquette de Peyret

LEFFE RUBY

Leffe Ruby was released onto the Belgian market in 2011, although it has been available in France for some time. It's a fruit beer that's part of the Leffe range, and this initially raised some eyebrows. Do abbeys and trappists brew fruit beers? It has become more commonplace for more variations to emerge from beneath the banner of a strong brand. Add Leffe Lentebier to the mix and you're left with a total of eight variants of the same brand. These are called line extensions in marketing terms. However, the fact of the matter is that it's not possible to undergo unlimited expansion without losing a certain amount of credibility.

Leffe Ruby is, at best, a pleasant fruit beer that is not too sweet. And that's about it.

Tasting

- *Origin: AB Inbev in Leuven*
- *Bottle: 33 cl with crown cap or 75 cl with cork stopper*
- *Alcohol content: 5% ABV*
- *Appearance: Clear beer with a red colour and light pink head.*
- *Nose: Pomegranate fragrance.*
- *Taste and aftertaste: Extremely feminine aperitif beer that tastes of raspberries.*

Mamé Vî Bleu

Visit to the fromagerie Gros Chène, Méan

We also came here to film our television programme. In his small cheese maker, Daniel Cloots makes delicious cheeses using fresh cows' or goats' milk sourced from surrounding farms. He only sells his cheese at the local market or to exclusive cheese shops. Every week, Michel sends his driver to buy some of these extraordinary cheeses that later appear on the tables of famous restaurants. Mamé vi is a very dry blue cheese. The *Penicillium roqueforti* is added to the curd in powder form, after which the cheese ripens in the cheese maker's cellar for a few weeks. Before it is ripened, it gets pierced so that its blue veins can develop.

Pairing

This was not an easy pairing. Michel had to return into his atelier a few times before he found the right match. An organic cheese made from raw cows' milk at the fromagerie Gros Chène in Méan finished off the job perfectly. The light, fruity beer guided and softened the dry, but very distinct, cheese and a successful marriage of flavours was achieved.

Alternative: Loblau

CHIMAY CINQ CENTS

Chimay Cinq Cents is probably the most underrated and least-known tripel in Flanders. Everyone swears by the Westmalle Tripel, but it's best to take note of its Walloon relative, because it is very, very good.

The famous Père Théodore developed this tripel during the 1960's. He chose just the right fermentations for it and, when the time came to celebrate the 500th anniversary of the city of Chimay, he decanted it into large 75 cl bottles. This celebratory beer was called 'Chimay Cinq Cents' and it was retained as part of the range.

Tasting

- **Origin:** *SA Bières de Chimay / Baileux*
- **Bottle:** *75 cl 'Belgian bottle' with champagne cork and blue muselet – the 33 cl version is called Chimay blanche – bottle fermented*
- **Alcohol content:** *8% ABV*
- **Appearance:** *Golden blond and crystal clear; slow carbonation supports a fine, white head that clings to the glass and is stable.*
- **Nose:** *Smoky and meaty, typical aroma of all Chimay beers – supplemented here with much hops bitterness and a touch of sulphur.*
- **Taste and aftertaste:** *Organic applies to this beer, because the flavour is made up of so many components. It has a herby bitterness and the alcohol is warming, though it has the same 'Hausgesmack' as does the rouge / première. This tripel is – literally – very strong, as its high alcohol content proves. Its aftertaste is lingering with a yeasty bitterness.*

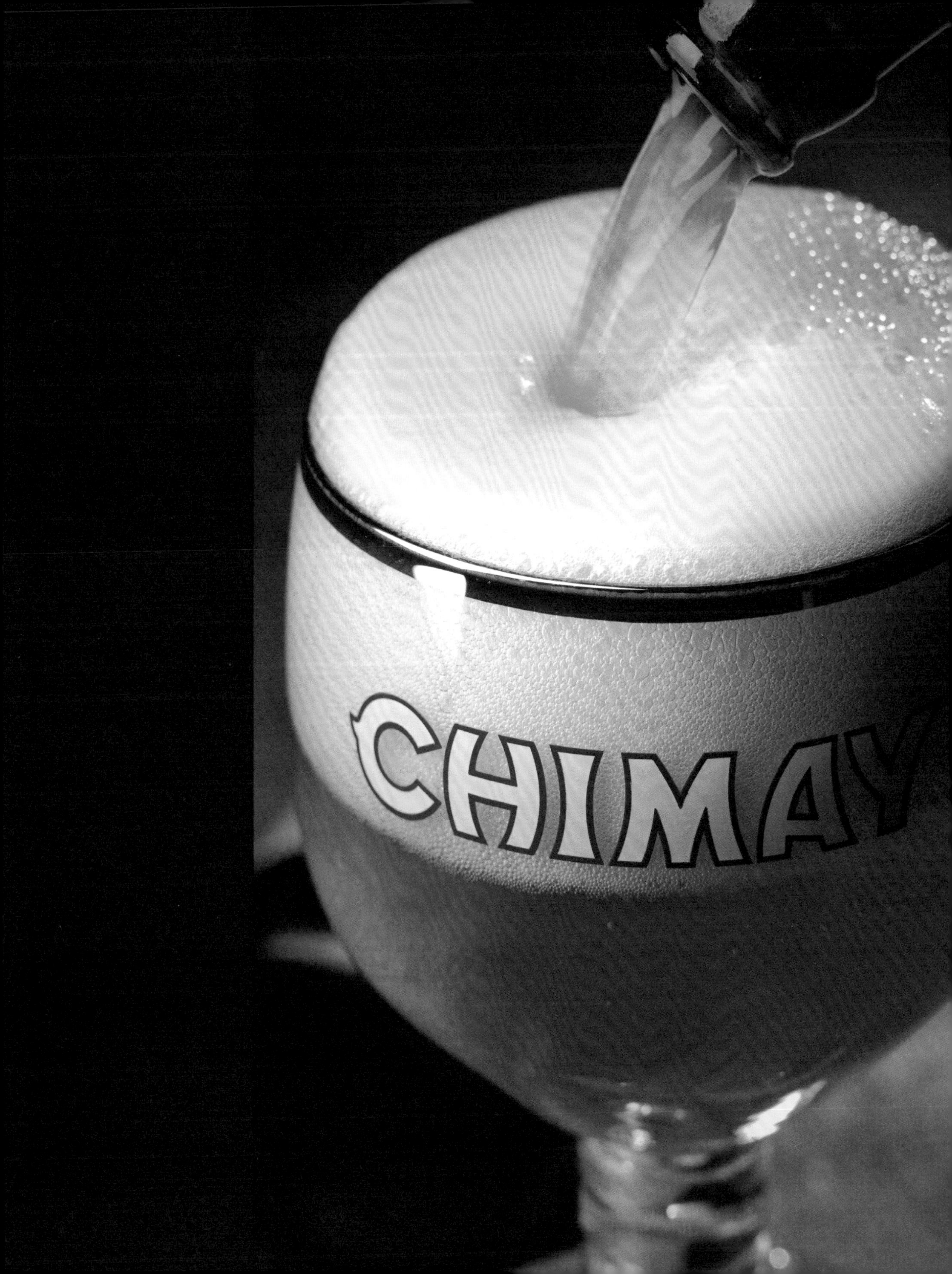
CHIMAY

Chimay à la Bière

Chimay cheese is a commercially-made cheese from Chimay. The milk used to produce it is collected from around 230 farmers in the region and is partially skimmed to 30 % and pasteurised. Then the milk is curdled and the curds cut. The whey is removed and cut into pieces of equal size. The cheese is then placed into moulds and pressed into its eventual shape. After being bathed in brine, it is placed in the ripening room, where the cheese develops its rind and is washed with Chimay trappist beer. This gives the cheese its distinct flavour.

Visit to the Chimay cheese maker

As part of our television series, Michel Van Tricht himself washed a Chimay a la Bière with beer. We were hosted by Le Potaupré, the inn not far from the abbey where one can taste all the beer and cheese produced by Chimay.

Pairing

Chimay à la Bière is smooth, distinctive and creamy – and very aromatic. It's a perfect match for the strong triple, as the chance visitors that we interviewed also discoverd.

Alternative: Stinking Bishop

HOPUS

This beer can easily be described as one of the trendsetters from the past few years. The Walloon Lefebvre brewery in Quenast – with the family's fifth generation at the helm – is better known for easily-accessible and commercial beers than it is for the Floreffe abbey beer range. The brewery also conducts a strong export trade, so its beer isn't commonplace within Belgium. Hopus, the well-hopped beer that son Pol-Emile developed during his brewing engineering studies, changed this. He served this beer at his wedding, and everyone enjoyed it so much that he added it to the fixed range. This distinctive blonde is a dream-come-true for any cheese pairing. Its characteristic bottle with swing-top reminds one of a rich brewing history.

Tasting

- *Origin: Lefebvre brewery, Quenast*
- *Bottle: 33 cl with swing-top*
- *Alcohol content: 8.5% ABV*
- *Appearance: Golden blonde with a thick head that clings to the glass.*
- *Nose: Floral, fresh with a dash of lemon.*
- *Taste and aftertaste: Full-bodied, initial smoothness with a rich hops flavour towards the end, very dry and thirst-quenching.*

Pouligny-Saint-Pierre AOP

A gorgeous goats' milk cheese in the shape of a pyramid from the eponymous village of Pouligny-Saint-Pierre in the Berry region in the Le Blanc district. It may be produced by co-operatives using predominantly pasteurised milk, and this origin is indicated by red labels. Farm-made cheeses have green labels and are always made using raw milk. Following a ripening period of five weeks, the rind acquires a natural mould while the cheese pate becomes soft and fine. The best 'fermier' cheeses are produced between May and October. This cheese is delicious when baked in the oven on some bread and accompanied by a fresh salad. One of the best Pouligny-Saint-Pierre fermiers is produced in very small quantities at the Ferme des Cabrioles in the Fontgombault.

Visit to Pouligny-Saint-Pierre

As part of our television series, we visited the farm belonging to the Reulier family in Fontgombault, the 'ferme des cabrioles', or the farm of the dancing goats. We had a great time relaxing on the grass amongst the goats and enjoying an 'Alexandre le bienheureux' moment. There are 150 goats on the farm that freely roam its 28 hectares and enjoy the fresh grass and herbs that grow on the pastures. And you can taste that! This is a very delicate cheese. Michel buys it at an age of twelve to thirteen days, after which he allows it to age for a further three to four weeks. The stunning pyramid shape is beautiful in itself and, after some time, the cheese also develops natural spots called 'flor naturelle'.

Pairing

To pair with this rich brewer's beer, Michel chose a tasty goats' milk cheese from the Loire named Pouligny-Saint-Pierre. This cheese is made on farms in the Berry region (Indre province) in 'La France Pofonde' from milk produced by goats that live on these farms. This is a heavenly pairing. The dry, fresh cheese rhymes – as it were – with the dry, bitter and rich beer.

Alternative: Torta del Casar

MAREDSOUS TRIPEL

The Maredsous range of abbey beers is somewhat underrated in the Belgian beer world. At Duvel-Moortgat, most attention is obviously paid to the main brand, although this has – to a certain extent – changed over the past few years. Maredsous has been notably restyled. Its packaging now has a very classy look that is more in keeping with the Benedictine monks, who were even involved in its design. The range includes a blonde, a brown and a tripel. We tasted the triple and also visited the Maredsous abbey itself in the village of Denée, not far from Dinant.

Tasting

- **Origin:** *Duvel-Moortgat, Breendonk*
- **Bottle:** *33 cl or 75 cl with cork stopper*
- **Alcohol content:** *8% ABV*
- **Appearance:** *Golden blonde, white and thick head.*
- **Nose:** *Fruity with hints of banana.*
- **Taste and aftertaste:** *Full-bodied and slightly herby, somewhat bitter aftertaste.*

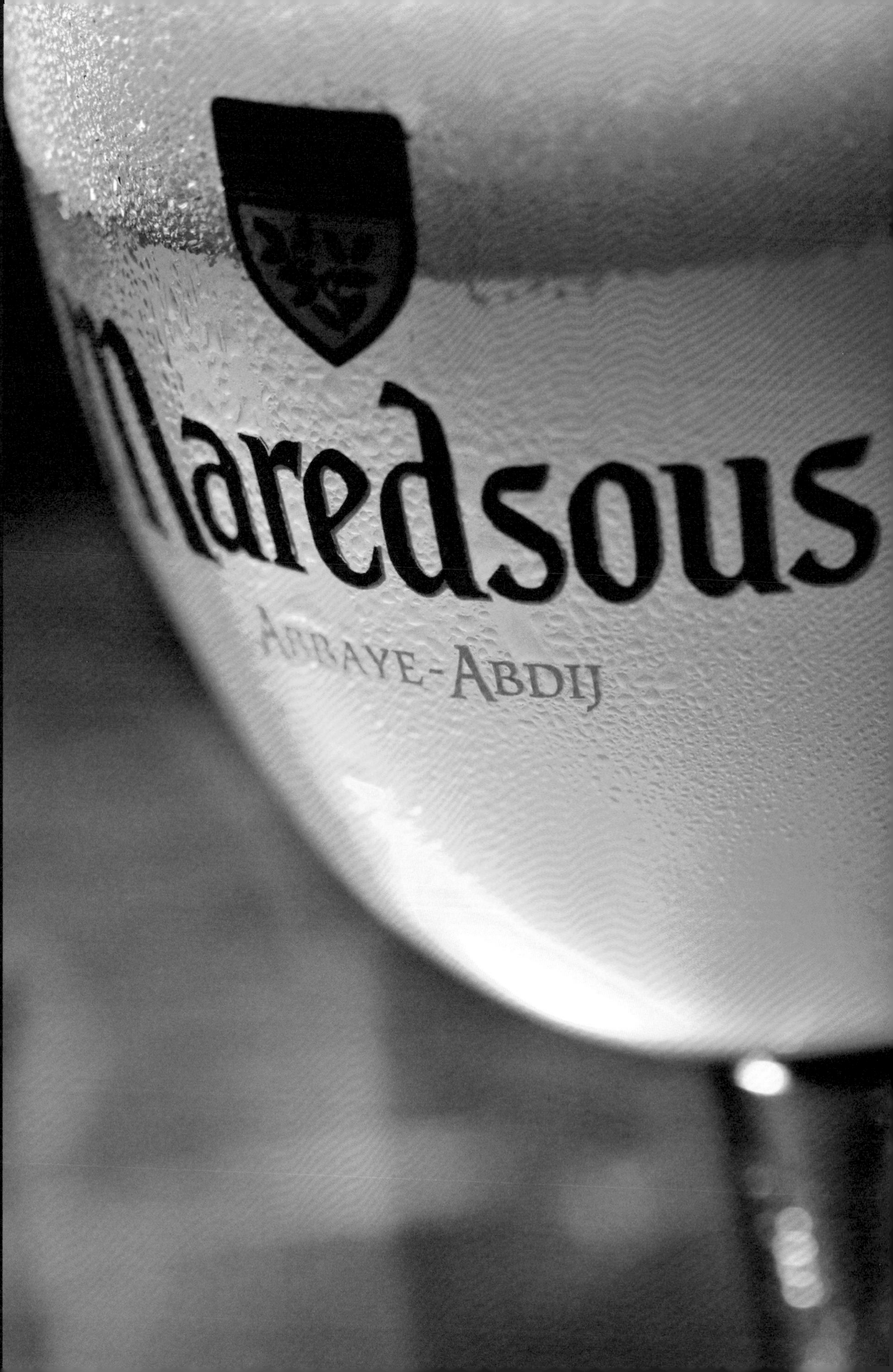
Maredsous
ABBAYE-ABDIJ

Maredsous Affiné

In 1953, the monks from the Maredsous abbey decided to start producing cheese. This seemed the obvious thing to do, given the large amounts of top-quality milk left over from their farmstead. They took inspiration from the well-known Port Salut cheese. Six years later, they handed over production to the Herve regional dairy and, later still, production became the responsibility of fromagerie Bel in France. This cheese is still ripened in the abbey's cellars, where the specific bacteria are found that give the cheese its characteristic taste. Even the water used to wash the rinds is re-used and contains the bacteria.

Visit to the Maredsous abbey

While filming our television programme, we enjoyed the privilege of visiting the abbey and the St. Joseph visitor's centre. The latter has been fully renovated and, every year, hosts around 400,000 foreign and domestic visitors. A guided tour, ending with a beer- and cheese tasting, is presented every day. We were personally guided around the abbey by Abbot Bernard Lorent. This Benedictine monetary has existed since 1872 and is a great example of neo-gothic architecture that perfectly blends into the surrounding green, rolling landscape. The abbey library holds more than 400,000 titles and the abbey's secret beer- and cheese recipes are also safeguarded here.

Pairing

Along with the Abbot, we tasted a combination of the Maredsous Tripel and a Maredsous cheese that had been ripened in the abbey for four months. We found the tripel to be even richer when combined with the cheese, and we relished a delicious sampling that the Abbot also enjoyed.

Alternative: Petit Basque

STRAFFE HENDRIK

As we mentioned previously, the Straffe Hendrik brand has returned to its roots, the Halve Maan brewery in Bruges. And it's become a 'straf (strong)' beer! This amber-coloured cracker has a rich Bruges history and can, once again, call itself the 'Brugs Stadsbier (Official beer of Bruges)' It is rich and creamy and begs to be paired with a cheese!

Tasting

- **Origin:** *De Halve Maan brewery / Bruges*
- **Bottle:** *33 cl apo bottle with crown cap – bottle fermented, or 75 cl with cork stopper.*
- **Alcohol content:** *9% ABV*
- **Appearance:** *Amber blonde or antique gold. Crystal clear with gradual, fine carbonation and a fine, white head that clings to the glass.*
- **Nose:** *Bitterness dominates, though caramel is also clearly present. Fragrance also contains hints of smokiness and meatiness.*
- **Taste and aftertaste:** *This strong Bruges beer comes across as fairly sweet on the palate due to a combination of alcohol (9% ABV is no low percentage) and malt. This beer tastes somewhat like the wort in the brewery, as though it hasn't undergone much fermentation. As a result, it is somewhat creamy. Hops, distinctive in the nose, doesn't follow through into the taste or the aftertaste. It's therefore a fairly one-dimensional beer and its short-lived aftertaste is like its flavour – nothing new develops.*

Brugse Blomme

This is a fairly new cheese. Belgomilk / Milcobel started producing this savoury cheese in 2002. Its special shape and the design on its rind come thanks to the ripening process, which takes place in cloths. Just like the Oud Brugge, it belongs to the Bruges family of cheeses and is made in the Moorslede in West-Flanders by Belgomilk, which uses pasteurised cows' milk to make this cheese.

Visit to De Halve Maan brewery

We visited De Halve Maan brewery along the Walplein near the Minnewater in the heart of Bruges to film part of our television series. It was a warm July day and, by noon, the courtyard was full of beer enthusiasts and tourists who had come to drink a 'Brugse Zot' or a 'Straffe Hendrik'. We interviewed brewer Xavier Vanneste on the roof of the brewery with its stunning views of Bruges. The tasting attracted a lot of attention. We got some of the tourists to taste our combination and they found it delicious!

Pairing

We discovered this amazing beer & cheese pairing during a tasting for the 'Bierpassie' magazine. Michel fully agreed with this combination. Brugse Blomme is a semi-hard cheese with an edible natural rind, creamy and smooth in texture and mild in flavour. The cheese dominates the beer in a pleasant way and does it justice. Both the beer and the cheese are characterised by the same creamy structure. On its own, the beer seems lighter than when combined with the cheese. Another aspect that counts in the favour of this pairing is that the beer and the cheese are both Bruges natives.

Alternative: Tomette de Chèvre

BOTTLE FERMENTED PALM

Everyone is familiar with Palm, Belgium's best-selling beer at one stage. During its heyday in 1998, the Steenhuffel brewery produced 700,000 hectolitres of beer. However, demand for 'special Belgian' beer tapered off and the brewery switched to a multi-niche strategy and concentrated on exports. Still, this is very pleasant, drinkable special beer. Perhaps it will even experience a revival now that its most significant rival, De Koninck, is making a comeback in the hands of highly-successful Duvel-Moortgat.

The Palm that we tasted is bottle fermented, something that always adds appeal.

Tasting

- *Origin: Palm Breweries, Steenhuffel*
- *Alcohol content: 5,4% ABV*
- *Nose: Fruity fermentation aroma, malty.*
- *Taste and aftertaste: Honey-like mellowness, fine and aromatic Kent hops create a subtle balance. Bottle fermentation ensures extra fruitiness, a delicious variant of the classic Palm beer.*

North Holland Gouda AOP

North Holland Gouda, with its red stamp*, is a cheese that credits its unique aromas to a unique soil type, the young and rich North Holland brackish sea clay. The grass that grows in this soil gives the cheese its natural, lightly salty flavour. The cheese is ripened on wooden boards and, the older the cheese, the more the sweet cheese flavour comes into its own and the more ripening crystals appear. The old version is ripened for at least ten months.

This cheese has been assigned a BOB or Beschermde Oorsprongsbenaming (Registered Source Name) because it's made using milk from North Holland cows, is made according to the original recipe and is ripened in North Holland. The red seal displays the emblem of the cheese porters, who – to this day – go about their business every Friday at the cheese market in Alkmaar.

Visit to the Alkmaar cheese market

We finished off our filming sessions with a visit to the cheese market in Alkmaar. Every Friday, between 1 April and the end of September, this totally unique event takes place. Approximately 30,000 kg of cheese is delivered to the market square and – as a show – is then sold, carried away by the cheese porters and weighed in the weighing room. Cheese maker, Fred Raaijmakers from FrieslandCampina let us in on some of the secrets of North Holland Gouda with its red seal. We tasted this superbly ripened cheese along with a strong bottle-fermented Palm on the patio of the Brouwersmuseum. This proved to be an elegant combination and the perfect conclusion to the book and the television series!

Pairing

We chose this pairing because both products are mild in flavour, but still have a lot of character. The fruity, bottle fermented Palm blends beautifully with the savoury, ripened cheese.

Alternative: Cabécou de Peyret

* Beschermde Oorsprongsbenaming (Registered Source Name) and registered brand name EU registration no. 3580974

Ben Vinken

BEN VINKEN | bIERSOMMELIER

Michel Van Tricht

MICHEL VAN TRICHT | KAASMEESTER